## Praise for *This Wide Te*

"The pilgrim moves through his days and informative guide, always in the n its two worlds—possessing a self who r another shadow self, drawn to the subterranean, who lives by his side. Hunt has written a mesmerizing, entrancing chronicle of the one who exists above the ground, and the one who is inexorably drawn to the world far below, where the Radium Girls still burn, where Ella Cruse lays crackling, where in Sicily's catacombs, riotous, celebratory, the dead in crepe and velvet beckon. In the midst of life and thinking and storytelling, 'thinking and dreaming gone to ruin.' A mysterious, often thrilling collection, beautifully done."
—**Carole Maso**

"Laird Hunt's *This Wide Terraqueous World* is a luminous gem of a book. Brimming with unexpected insights at every turn—whether visiting W. G. Sebald's grave or Willa Cather's Red Cloud or observing donkeys at a distance in China, Corsica, California—here is an account of a writer's life in which verifiable truths and an unfettered imagination work together brilliantly. Acting as a kind of post-postmodern Virgil, Hunt takes us on a journey in which travelogue melds with philosophy, literary acumen informs cultural observation, and far-ranging memories are set free by an unusually prodigious curiosity about every large and little thing. A kaleidoscope of genre-defying essays that leaves the reader frankly awestruck, *This Wide Terraqueous World* is a book to celebrate and treasure."
—**Bradford Morrow**

"Heads or Tails? An ancient game of chance. And what of the middle, the space between the head and tail? If it is, it is in the flip; it is in the moment of the coin glinting in its unfixed oscillation amidst this radiant uncertainty. It is here that I locate Laird Hunt's visionary prose. Between the uncanny crisp edge of the detail and the blurred seam where a scene once collected, between remembering and forgetting, between the self and the act of writing, between the painted tiles that decorated the childhood nursery and those that now punctuate the scene of language's attempts, there is something, but what? Love, like a fact. How strange—that we get to be here. A stunning master class in both awareness and exquisite prose, *This Wide Terraqueous World* reminds us that Laird Hunt is one of the greatest writers of our time."
—**Selah Saterstrom**

# THIS WIDE TERRAQUEOUS WORLD

ALSO BY LAIRD HUNT

# THIS WIDE
# TERRAQUEOUS
# WORLD

Laird Hunt

**COFFEE HOUSE PRESS**
Minneapolis
2023

Coffee House Press books are available to the trade through our primary distributor, Consortium Book Sales & Distribution, cbsd.com or (800) 283-3572. For personal orders, catalogs, or other information, write to info@coffeehousepress.org.

Coffee House Press is a nonprofit literary publishing house. Support from private foundations, corporate giving programs, government programs, and generous individuals helps make the publication of our books possible. We gratefully acknowledge their support in detail in the back of this book.

LIBRARY OF CONGRESS CATALOGING-IN-PUBLICATION DATA

Names: Hunt, Laird, author.
Title: This wide terraqueous world / Laird Hunt.
Other titles: This wide terraqueous world (Compilation)
Description: Minneapolis : Coffee House Press, 2023.
Identifiers: LCCN 2022039200 (print) | LCCN 2022039201 (ebook) | ISBN 9781566896672 (paperback) | ISBN 9781566896689 (epub)
Subjects: LCGFT: Essays.
Classification: LCC PS3608.U58 T48 2023 (print) | LCC PS3608.U58 (ebook) | DDC 814/.6—dc23/eng/20221116
LC record available at https://lccn.loc.gov/2022039200
LC ebook record available at https://lccn.loc.gov/2022039201

PRINTED IN THE UNITED STATES OF AMERICA

30  29  28  27  26  25  24  23          1  2  3  4  5  6  7  8

*It is not for nothing that the reels in our minds start*
*revolving at a speed we might find difficult to bear.*
—Azareen Van der Vliet Oloomi

*Même si c'est un drôle de cadeau, je remercie mon père*
*et ma mère de m'avoir donné la vie.*
—Édouard Levé

# CONTENTS

# THIS WIDE TERRAQUEOUS WORLD

# TIGER [TIGER] TIGER

*Somewhere during my first or second year a tiger came into my life. It lived in bright paint on three more or less standard-sized tiles. My mother mounted them in my room. This was in Singapore. The late 1960s. That was the life. We went to the botanical gardens. We swam in turquoise pools. It was always hot. We had a Doberman pinscher named Sinta. My parents went to and hosted cocktail parties. Somewhere out there the guns and bombs of the Vietnam War were booming. My father was doing business for an American bank. He spent months away from us embedded in the routine amazements of Jakarta. He was on active reserve, expected to be called up, never was. I spoke a local dialect of Chinese better than I spoke English. The war wound down. We moved. I developed a pronounced English accent as a small boy in London. Later, I skated on frozen Dutch canals. One of the tiles the tiger was painted on didn't make it through these adventures. My mother put the two remaining tiles in a box.*

*Years and years later she sent them to me. I unwrapped them and looked at them, then hammered some nails into the wall and put them up next to my writing desk. They live in my house. I can see them from where I'm sitting.*

*In the Cluny Museum in Paris, hanging in fragments on the wall in one of the first rooms, are the remnants of a fine gown from the late Middle Ages.*

The last time I visited the museum, the ghost of the rest of the dress hung on the wall around the fragments. A small woman was walking up behind me to take her dress down off the wall and put it on. One shivers at such times. When contemplating ghost dresses. When contemplating fragments with ghosts swarming the surround.

In the prologue to Junky, William S. Burroughs writes, "My earliest memories are colored by a fear of nightmares. I was afraid to be alone, and afraid of the dark, and afraid to go to sleep because of dreams where a supernatural horror seemed always on the point of taking shape. I was afraid some day the dream would still be there when I woke up."

I woke up. It was Singapore, circa 1970. I looked out through the bars of my crib. There was a tile floor. Gauze covering the window. The tiger was in the room.

There are monsters that can do all sorts of things. Monsters that will drag you into the air or pull you deep underground. There are monsters that will prick your finger, others that will tear off your arm. Some monsters stand snarling before you. Some monsters have "for the children" painted on their flanks. Others hide like Poe's purloined letter in plain sight. Some monsters make it their business to swallow the world.

Let me describe this tiger as it is now. It is mouth without stomach. Face without eyes. Legs without heart. Tail without teeth. Teeth without claws.

Once my tiger had a stomach. Once it had a heart. My tiger is hungry without its stomach, always hungry. I always hold its tiles by their edges. I imagine I do myself some good by keeping its two halves separated. I imagine a lot of things.

Burroughs once wrote a story called "Tiger in the Valley." The story is lost. No one quite knows how it went. The story may have been based on so-called actual events. A bar in Mexico kept a lion in a pit out back. A man got drunk and decided to show his friends how to pet the lion. The lion tore the man apart. Burroughs tore the story apart and turned the lion into a tiger and wrote it down. Then it got lost.

I had an anthropology professor in college who liked to illustrate his points with vivid images. One of his points was that people, not the rest of the animal kingdom, have the market cornered on the monstrous. His illustration involved a lion and a chick. The setting was an African lion sanctuary. A young man or a young woman was holding a chick and thought it was adorable. This young person got the idea that a nearby lion must find the chick adorable as well. He or she therefore slipped the chick through the bars of the enclosure so the lion could admire it. The lion looked at the chick, sniffed it, then very matter-of-factly bit off its head.

Like my anthropology professor, I don't believe that actual lions and tigers are monstrous. Very, very good at what they do being more like it. But I do believe that my eyeless tile tiger, which looks for all the world like it sprung straight out of the pages of Borges's **Book of Imaginary Beings**, or out of one of Hieronymus Bosch's bubbling pools, or out of one of Burroughs's nightmares, is a monster. I'm very attached to it. I've spent a great deal of time trying to write its heart, uncoil its innards, pump oxygen into its vanished lungs, give it back those eyes.

We know what Blake had to say about Tygers.
"A tiger comes to mind," Borges wrote.

*It has occurred to me to wonder what will happen if I lose another tile. If all I have left are haunches and tail. If all I have left are jaws and teeth. Of course one day I will lose them all. Or they will be lost to me.*

*On the back of each tile is a logo and a stamp that reads "Made in Japan."*

*Recently my mother told me that there were never three tiles. That she had seen the two tiles and liked the look of them. A tiger without its middle.*

*History is fiction. Fiction is history.*

*Fair enough.*

# UN STORY

At the United Nations around the end of the last millennium, identity cards were worn around the neck, most generally strung on cheap beaded chains. The cards were made by UN security guards at a facility across the street from the main complex. If the guard taking your photograph was nice, he or she would let you see the picture before hitting print. Most of my pictures were pretty good. During the five years I worked at the United Nations, I accumulated a considerable number of these cards. I still have most of them. In a plastic bag somewhere in the basement.

I don't know if one was required to wear identity cards at the CIA. When one was at headquarters in Langley, Virginia, I mean. Obviously a CIA officer, in the field, would not have worn an identity card.

A low-level United Nations employee on duty in the field would.

When I was sent to cover the signing of the United Nations Convention against Transnational Organized Crime, in Palermo, I wore my identity card as I walked down the middle of the main thoroughfares, which had been fenced off for the occasion. There we went, alone or in groups, down the empty streets.

I liked to walk down the empty streets. Much of the coverage I was doing was of a subsidiary committee meeting in a twelfth-century Norman palace on the far side of town. The walk took around half an hour. There were parks to negotiate as well as the empty streets. Light came through the trees and children played on the swept gravel. Away from the town center life went on uninterrupted. I would leave my hotel early so I could take my time. On the return, though, when I had reentered the town center and was walking along the blocked-off avenues, I felt the urge to hurry, to look purposive. Back at the hotel I would ring up to my colleague's room and see if he wanted to come down to the little bar for a drink. Usually he was there and did. We drank Campari without soda or lemon or we drank underchilled Italian beer. The lobby around us was swarmed with armed policemen. Some carried machine guns. They were a gregarious bunch. Young and rather bored now that the whole thing was underway and no one was being killed.

*Not yet,* we thought.

In the evenings the streets were opened up again and the cars went rushing along and we took off our identity cards and our ties and went out to look around.

I never went to CIA headquarters in Langley, Virginia, for the final stage of the yearlong hiring process that would likely have made me an intelligence officer for the agency. All that remained, after the series of tests I had taken and interviews I had undergone, was to visit Langley and submit myself to a physical exam and a lie-detector test. I reached the stage in the proceedings where a young woman called me to make arrangements for my visit. That in the end I chose not to undertake the voyage laid out for me was looked upon philosophically by my deep-voiced recruiting contact. "All right, Mr. Hunt," he said. He gave me a number, in the event that I changed my mind, and bid me farewell and good luck in Japan (where I had decided to spend a year teaching English).

The CIA had invited me, when I was a senior at Indiana University, to take a series of aptitude tests that would help them to determine whether, as my profile indicated, I was suitable agency material. Apparently, a chipper high-voiced CIA recruitment officer told me in a dingy hotel room in Indianapolis after I had gone through the aptitude tests, I was. And how. She was, she told me, honestly impressed. In light of my success on the exams, the agency had every reason to think I would make a very, very good CIA officer. One who would work in the field.

I have always liked to read.

When I was on mission in Palermo I was reading a novel by Jane Bowles. I was reading this novel by Jane Bowles and thinking of the writing of her onetime husband, Paul Bowles, whose work had moved me deeply some years before. Progressively, as I read the novel by Jane Bowles, I thought less of the writing of Paul Bowles. The writing of Jane Bowles began to sizzle on the page before me. The writing of Jane Bowles seemed at moments of intensity to have something in common with tectonic shear and uplift, to become, as I wrote in the notebook

I was keeping on that trip, a bewilderment of unbearable heat. I had a nice bright top-floor hotel room with a balcony that gave me a view of the rooftops of Palermo, and during my spare moments, when I needed to catch my breath, I let this novel by Jane Bowles sizzle both on the page and in my eyes and also somewhere down in the dark, there where the cosmos keeps fierce council, and afterward, when I went out walking, or just went down to the lobby for another Campari, which in addition to lacking soda and lemon was presented without ice, some of what Bowles was doing and describing in her novel spilled out into the world around me.

That texture of a world that was not the world.

A kind of ectoplasm stuck to walls and barstools.

One of the policemen with a machine gun told me I ought to go and see the Capuchin Catacombs if I had some spare time. That if I was really interested in seeing something special I ought to go there. I told him I had been to the catacombs in Paris and walked the long corridors and seen the skulls and bones piled up to the ceiling, but he just smiled and said the two could not be compared.

We had received some tips from more experienced colleagues on where, in the evening, to get a nice glass of dark Sicilian wine and where to get some nice rich Sicilian sausage. To get to this place, quite popular with the chic set of Palermo, we had to walk down narrow winding streets in the dusk light. We did not wear our United Nations identity cards on this walk and the others we took. As I have already mentioned. There were rumors going around the UN staff that La Cosa Nostra had it in mind to shoot some of us. So the idea was that we shouldn't, when we were off duty, draw any particular attention to ourselves, even if we had spent much of the day doing just that.

Palermo seemed to be crumbling. The facades of many buildings were dark from soot. Others were being knocked down. I found a number of pieces of handsome tile in a dumpster. I wrapped them in a napkin and put them in my jacket pocket. I still have them. I also still have one of the two hand-painted espresso cups I got at a pottery store on my last day. The Guyanese colleague I went around with in Palermo, for his part, bought himself "a nice piece of leather." It did not look so very nice to me, but then perhaps my espresso cups and jar of Sicilian marmalade and tiles plucked from a dumpster had not impressed him, so I said nothing but agreeable things when he asked my opinion.

The CIA would have asked me to lie. They would have asked me to lie about what I did to everyone except my closest family. I would have been, so the high-voiced recruiter at the dingy hotel room in Indianapolis explained it to me, a low- to midlevel functionary at a foreign embassy, at least in the eyes of the world. Such a position would have been my cover. "You're a failure," the world would have declared. While secretly . . .

Not long ago I saw a movie where an outwardly mild-mannered CIA employee brutally stabs someone in the stomach on a dark, winding street much like the ones we negotiated to reach our wine bar that night in Palermo. He stabs the person and drops the knife and walks on.

I got my job at the UN through a friend of a friend. That friend of a friend became a kind of friend in his own right but then he left the UN and I lost touch with him. Our office was just outside the Security Council. Every morning I went up the escalator and got a view of Picasso's *Guernica* tapestry.

There were those who thought, when I was working at the United Nations, that I was actually working for the CIA. The poet Bernadette Mayer was one of these people. It was sort of a joke, but it was a joke that went on for some years.

I was another of these people. I mean at moments.

Walking down the darkening, narrow street in Palermo with my identity card tucked into my pocket, a French Canadian and a Guyanese colleague on either side of me, was one of these moments. I had grown a goatee for the trip and someone, looking at me, had said my goatee looked like a disguise.

No one got shot during that mission. The United Nations Convention against Transnational Organized Crime got signed. I had my drink with my colleagues at the wine bar. I bought some souvenirs. I never joined the CIA. The young French Canadian woman stayed on at the UN and was later crushed to death in a stairwell in Haiti. I went home.

This story, such as it is, ends in the famous Capuchin Catacombs beneath the streets of Palermo where (as the machine gun–toting policeman had told me) for two hundred years the wealthy dead of the city were set on display. They are, most of them, still there. In their crepe dresses, in their purple velvet pants, in their priestly robes. Rosalia Lombardo, who died at age two on December 6, 1920, and was one of the last corpses to be interred in the catacombs before the local authorities banned the practice, can be found tucked into a little bed. Nicknamed "Sleeping Beauty," Rosalia's body is still perfectly intact. Embalmed by a certain Alfredo Salafia, she is in a glass case, looking very much like a surreal doll. There is also a baby lying nearby on a yellow blanket. The baby does not look like a doll.

Recently I read Giuseppe di Lampedusa's great novel of Sicily, *The Leopard,* which is partially set in Palermo. Nowhere in the novel, written half a century after the events it treats, are the catacombs mentioned, although the nineteenth century would have been their heyday. Dust, on the other hand, is everywhere in the novel, dust and smoke and ash.

•

# GIRAFFE STORY

In early November 2010, my wife, Eleni, my daughter, Eva, and I traveled by high-speed train from Paris to London. The trip over was uneventful. A tall woman in a suit gave up her seat so the three of us could sit together. When five-year-old Eva grew bored we took walks in the aisle and played games in the dining car. It was night outside so there was nothing to see. The train ran late. I was thinking a lot about giraffes at the time. For part of the trip Eva looked at her portable DVD player. I kept having warm feelings about giraffes, though I didn't really know very much about them. Our friend Chiaki met us at St. Pancras and we took a taxi to Islington, where we had a place to stay.

The flat was small and cold and the next few days were rainy. The flat had a very small bathroom with a tub you got into by clambering over the toilet. We very quickly broke the fragile light string and had to use a flashlight when we made our ablutions. There was carpet on the floor of the apartment. The kitchen was narrow. It all felt very familiar.

I had lived in London twice as a boy and took considerable pleasure in the waves of nostalgia that kept sweeping over me. For example, when I would pass a low dark brick wall with rain dripping on it. Or when I would see a packet of Rowntree's Fruit Pastilles for sale in the Underground. Black currant had been my favorite variety of pastille. We had had vague thoughts of taking Eva to the London Zoo, where I went often as a child, and where perhaps I could see and photograph a live giraffe, but the rain put paid to that. I had especially loved entering the giant net of the aviary at the zoo. This would have been in 1974 or '75. Entering that huge space full of birds that couldn't fly too far away from me.

I went to Saint Christina's School as a small boy and lived in St. John's Wood. Later I went to the American School in London and, later still, on another occasion, went again to the American School in London and lived in South Kensington. There are not great quantities of sunshine associated with the memories I have of these periods. Though I do recall playing in mossy gardens and pitching in baseball games in Regent's Park. I had a girlfriend named Wendy and did some sloppy kissing. After a particularly painful round of this sloppy kissing, Wendy told me that her mother had said we must break up. I was in the Boy Scouts. I had a friend named Benny. Once some of my other friends went boating and got very wet together to their great preteen glee but I was not, alas, with them that day.

We liked Paris a great deal that fall and London suffered a bit by comparison. The houses looked small and socked in, like children set to carry heavy loads in some novel that should have long since been laid to rest. The streets were narrow but not curving. The shopwindows were not elegant. We were not interested, at that moment, in being down with general drear and shopwindow shab. Please do not imagine that I am proud of this.

We enjoyed reading in the William IV on Shepherdess Walk though. It was an old pub. A festive group had gathered. Eva helped us give our readings for a while, then retreated to her DVDs at the back of the room. This did not seem to us to be a failure in parenting as we had readings to get on with. Professional obligation and so forth. Eva watched a Miyazaki video. Or perhaps it was Felix the Cat. We did not drink beer. Heavy glasses of excellent dark red wine were put into our hands. One of the people who had attended the reading—a poet who has since left us—went down to get his friends' drinks and in his drunkenness dropped a whole tray of beverages onto the floor. One of our dearest old friends was in the room. Eva and I went outside afterward and took photos of each other. I became momentarily annoyed when she bonked my camera into a bench she was climbing. The camera, an Olympus PEN E-PL1, was O.K. Eva apologized for bonking it and I accepted her apology even though when you are five and it is late in the evening in London and your father lets you hang an expensive camera around your neck while both of you are running back and forth across the quiet street, nothing in the situation is your fault.

I suspect my own father, who used to take my sister and me on weekend outings around London and in the surrounding countryside in the distant 1970s, would have seen it the same way. My father was branch manager for a large bank in those days. He vanished off into his world in the morning and reappeared in the evening. This was around the heyday of the musical *Jesus Christ Superstar*. I am trying now to understand why my sister and I, five and seven at the time, listened often enough to an LP of the production to have it memorized. "Christ! I know you can't hear me, but I only did what you wanted me to. . . ." This was also the period of my father's great interest in the guitar. He played it often in the evening and took lessons from a young man who would come to the house. Of course my father was a young man then too. He played the guitar to us at night before bedtime. He sang stories to us. I wish I had a recording of one of them, and of the soft little beats of our breaths in the background, but I do not. The world does not offer itself to us this way. Not often at any rate. I suspect I was happy when my father was playing to us before bedtime. Insofar as happy encompasses all the emotions when we are very young. Rage, fear, madness, delight. There we go lying alone in our bodies in the dark.

Then the next day we went to the British Museum. Or had we already gone there? Regardless, I took Eva to see Ginger, who died and was buried in Egyptian sand 5,500 years ago, just as my mother, on one of her good days, many years earlier, had taken me and my sister to see Ginger soon after he was brought to the museum. I had forgotten that Ginger, so nicknamed because of the ginger patch of hair that remains on his head, is a desiccated corpse curled up in his ancient skin and that some of Ginger's inner organs seem to protrude from between his legs. I had forgotten, I suppose I mean, that Ginger is frightening. That Ginger lies surrounded by funereal pots that signify, as Ginger himself does, the terrifyingly old, the long-vanished, whole ecosystems of thinking and dreaming grown to ruin. Eva expressed her desire for me not to die soon after we saw Ginger. I won't, I said to her. Not yet. I promise. We did not show her the strangely beautiful crushed warrior and princess heads that were close to Ginger's case. Crushed by the weight of the earth caving in on their burial sites. Instead we took her down to see the Elgin Marbles, where she sat in the gray-blue light, sketching long past the ordinary confines of her attention span.

One afternoon during the trip, I went with Andrew, a former student and now a friend, to visit the Soane's Museum, which houses a collection of modest antiquities that gradually, as you drift past them, accumulate into something extraordinary. Room after strange unsettling room is lined with stone remnants or plaster representations of Greek and Roman objects. A sarcophagus sits in state in one of the basement chambers and everywhere candles shimmer on snapped-off columns and temple shards. There are other things too at the Soane's Museum—more recent paintings and clocks and carpets—but it is all the gray bits hanging on the walls that I think of now when I shut my eyes. Afterward, Andrew and I walked through Lincoln's Inn and made our way to one of Andrew's old beverage haunts, from his days as a literary fiction editor, where we sat in a dark booth and drank each other's health and spoke, if I remember correctly, about reading apps that stood a good chance of bringing the much-maligned novella (too long to stand in easy company with other pieces;

too short, absent a brand-name author behind them, to stand alone) back into the public eye.

People regularly kill giraffes.

They do this despite the fact that *they are even-toed ungulate mammals, the tallest of all land-living animal species, and the largest ruminants. The giraffe's scientific name, which is similar to its antiquated English name of camelopard, refers to its irregular patches of color on a light background and bears a token resemblance to a leopard's spots. The average mass for an adult male giraffe is 1,200 kilograms (2,600 pounds) while the average mass for an adult female is 830 kilograms (1,800 pounds). It is approximately 4.3 meters (14 feet) to 5.2 meters (17 feet) tall, although the tallest male recorded stood almost 6 meters (20 feet)* according, accurately or inaccurately, to Wikipedia (which may have updated its entry since I first drafted this), where I spend more time these days than I do in my once much-thumbed *Columbia Encyclopedia*—so heavy and handsome in its 1945 single-volume edition. I bought it during the period when I was just setting out to sea as a writer, a period during which I couldn't resist the reassuring solidity of old volumes that had withstood the various grudges of time. I still have many a Modern Library hardcover—red and blue, gray and green—sitting on shelves in the basement. The *Columbia Encyclopedia*, for its part, is upstairs in the back room, but it is lying on its side, spine in or out, and I know that it is buried.

Zarafa, who during the nineteenth century lived for many years in the Jardin des Plantes in Paris, and who has stood, stuffed, for many more years now, in a museum in La Rochelle, which Eleni once visited, was never buried so does not now lie in some hidden giraffe cemetery on the savanna, nothing more than a jumble of hyena-scraped bones. Or the dust of bones. Scattered hither and thither. Zarafa died, and was stuffed, a long time ago.

Despite all this, in the evenings, after he had finished teaching, our dear old friend Tim, who is married to Chiaki, would come to the flat and have dinner with us. We talked about poetry and the shit state of British papers and the dreariness of London. This was the period when the Chilean miners were still trapped deep underground and though we had little to say on the subject I believe it came up in our gestures and glances. I don't think I brought up giraffes but I might have. We ate takeout fish and chips and Indian food. Tim and Eleni would walk out to get the food we had ordered while Eva and I stayed behind. The flat had a small but good selection of interesting but not easy avant-garde jazz and classical music. Eva and I did not listen to this. One evening we had huge amounts of pungent leftovers, but Tim did not want to take it on the Underground with him for fear, he said quite reasonably, of stinking up the Tube car. In consequence, I dumped, then rinsed each plastic container and took them out to the recycling bin. It was cool and rainy outside. Wind blew through trees that had not yet lost all their leaves.

The last time I lived in England, Margaret Thatcher was prime minister and the Yorkshire Ripper was in the news. I took the Tube to school. I had friends and we ran around London together in the afternoons. I remember once going to Billingsgate Fish Market with my father and stepmother and taking a live eel home in a plastic bag filled with water. We ate that eel for dinner and so its molecules became ours. I have had many dreams in which I was underwater and understood that even in the dream it would be impossible to breathe. The dreams, not quite a series, though there are several of them, have been about this understanding. This understanding that I will not be able to breathe when I am dead.

Tim's eldest daughter, Koto, was sick so we didn't see her during our visit. Tim's younger daughter, Yuki, was also ailing but recovered and we saw her our last morning—at the Gagosian Britannia Street gallery where we went to take a look at a James Turrell show. The main piece in the show was a cave of shifting light into which we stepped without our shoes. The cave seemed to have no ending even when we walked right up to it. The gallery we had stepped out of looked like a photograph when seen from inside the cave. Yuki was very young and her eyes gleamed as the light shifted from violet to pink. I tried to think of how a novel could do what the light was doing in that curvy space and in Yuki's eyes but could not. Novels are like huge, inefficient engines. They are really the worst. It would have been very hard for a giraffe to enter the cave. Eleni and Eva had been to Turrell's volcano, the famous Roden Crater, where Eleni had participated in a poetry reading, so we discussed that a bit. This and that, we said. A gallery employee very pleasantly hurried us along.

After the show we had pizza in a restaurant opposite the British Library, which stands next to St. Pancras station. Before we went to the station, which was crowded but calm, we stopped in the library and saw the permanent exhibit of manuscripts and listened to a recording of Virginia Woolf reading from *Mrs. Dalloway. Mrs. Dalloway* is my favorite novel by Virginia Woolf. There is nothing inefficient about *Mrs. Dalloway.* Virginia Woolf would have known what to do with Turrell's cave. The opening pages of *Mrs. Dalloway* are full of light. I like those pages better than almost anything. After we had seen the exhibit we said goodbye to Tim, Chiaki, and Yuki, who may by this time have fallen asleep in her stroller, at the entrance to St. Pancras and made our way back to Paris.

This did not keep me, two days earlier, from getting up while Eva and Eleni were still asleep and taking the Tube to Liverpool Street where I purchased a ticket for the 8 a.m. train to Norwich, in East Anglia, nor from taking a taxi, once I had arrived in Norwich, after a train ride spent constructing a small review of the New Directions rerelease of Sir Thomas Browne's *Urn Burial,* to the village of Framingham Earl, and more specifically the churchyard attached to St. Andrews, a thirteenth-century structure where I paid my respects at the grave of W. G. Sebald, who died in 2001. It was a cool but sunny morning. The churchyard was deserted. It took about five minutes to find Sebald's grave. My predecessors had lined up pebbles on the top of the thin rectangle of slate onto which his name had been carved. A vase of flowers sat at its base. The churchyard was very pretty. Birds sang. Branches moved in the breeze. The ground was spongy. I took photos of the grave.

Later, trying to find a bus stop, I asked a woman walking her small dog how to get to Framingham Earl. She scrunched up her face and told me that I was in

Framingham Earl. I asked her where, then, I could find Poringland. She told me I was practically there too. That it was all, including Framingham Pigot, more or less the same place. Even though each place, of course, was different. I walked on. I took a double-decker bus out of the towns of Framingham Earl, Framingham Pigot, and Poringland, which Sebald would have known well, since he lived in their environs for twenty-five years, and it was where he died in a car crash, apparently following a cardiac arrest, and back into Norwich, which he would have also known well, where I spent the remainder of the morning and early afternoon walking the streets. I was not at all unaware as I walked that all Sebald's books feature walkers of one stripe or another, nor was I unfamiliar with his frequent allusions to ghosts, doubles, and full-fledged doppelgangers, and as I walked I kept a lookout for deceptively dour-faced, robustly mustached, bespectacled men of a certain age, also out walking the thoroughfares and noticing the cracks in the streets, which for all they knew and perhaps because of it, might give onto bottomless chasms, and saw not a few of them.

I saw another one, standing outside the Boulder coffee shop where I once sat typing this. They are everywhere. Even though Sebald is dead and will continue to be, just as Sir Thomas Browne, whose statue presides over Hay Hill in the center of Norwich, and whose remains lie beneath the stone floor in the nearby church of St. Peter Mancroft, which in turn sits very near Browne's long-since-demolished seventeenth-century lodgings, is dead and will continue to be. There are other memorials to Browne on Hay Hill. These include a sculpture of a giant brain and seating areas inscribed with some of his most famous titles. A pair of Spanish-speaking visitors had their picture taken next to the brain while I was there. I took a picture of the brain too. Before I left Norwich I had lunch in a Thai restaurant. The food was quite good but the portions a bit small.

Something I thought of more often than I might have liked in the following days in London and after our return to Paris, where our time was coming to an end, and where in the final weeks before we went home to Colorado I was happy to make myself available to help publicize the French edition of my third novel, *The Exquisite,* a book that owes a significant, if curiously configured, debt to Sebald, a fact I address in that novel's afterword, which I understand serves both to clarify and confuse.

My giraffe thinking went nowhere.

Where does thinking go?

At one point, when I was taking pictures of Sebald's grave, I found myself lying on my side on the ground that covers his coffin.

I leapt up and brushed off my pants.

Everyone knows the dead can break loose. That they can come for us whenever they like.

Still, it may or may not be, because Ginger was so clearly not going to get up and lark about (though one wonders if the dreams of people who have seen him would put the lie to this) that Eva broke into dance in the main lobby at the base of the curling staircase in the British Museum soon after we had looked into Ginger's glass enclosure. There was something vaguely Egyptian in her dance. Also something kind of kung fu.

There is more to be said about all this but of course it will not be said.

World, you visited me every day.

World, I kept wondering about you.

# HALF MOON
(a provisional fiction)


In "The Approach to Al-Mu'tasim," by Jorge Luis
Borges, a man spends his youth searching for the divine.
He sees its echoes in many of the people he encounters.
Once his youth and adventures are over, the man steps
through a door and finds what he has been looking for.
It is not clear whether this is supposed to be happy, this
ending.

Recently I dreamed that the devil was leading me astray,
then helping me, then leading me astray again, then
both at the same time. My dream had two levels. The
action occurred in the first and the explaining in the
second. I wasn't sure what there was left for me to do
when I woke up.

Feel, I thought. I am supposed to feel.

Action, explain, feel.

The dream involved an elevator shaft, some kind of control panel, a towel dispenser, toothpicks. The idea of the

first part of the dream, as explained by me to some witness (maybe the devil) in the second, was that as long as I did all my habitual actions, clues would be revealed. If I missed a habitual action, say forgot to pull a towel out of the towel dispenser after I washed my hands in the public toilet, a clue would be irreversibly lost. What I was supposed to solve by gathering clues was unclear.

When I woke I felt unsettled, excited.

Feeling.

But of course I may have been wrong. It's quite possible, of course, that what I was supposed to do when I woke was run.

I tend to be uninspired by eventualities. This may be what keeps me from being an entirely effective novelist. Or an entirely effective builder of short stories. Or of poems.

Not that I ever try to write poems. Not anymore. There was a time in my early twenties when I tried. Oh man. Recently, reading a Jack Spicer chapbook, a gorgeous thing designed by the printer Wesley Tanner, reading lines like "Love ate the red wheelbarrow," I thought maybe I should have fucking kept at it.

I am not necessarily the biggest Jack Spicer fan. But that little book . . .

Borges doesn't spell out what the man in "The Approach to Al-Mu'tasim" discovers when he steps through the door. He provides some hints, some vectors, some flares. The story is presented in the form of a book review. Properly speaking, then, the story is not about the man and his search at all: it is about a nonexistent novel: which is to say it is about literature: language: nonexistence: immanence.

Words.

Speaking of words: "No money, no honey," a series of young men said to us as they led us through the hot streets of Marrakech, Morocco, toward the city tanneries. They smiled when they said this. This was a while ago. Not long after our visit to London. I was walking with Eva on my shoulders. It was a sort of mini-epic walk. You could smell the tanneries long before you got to them. When we arrived, our final guide handed us the "gas masks" he had promised during the latter portion of our trek. The gas masks were sprigs of mint. Surprisingly effective, but still. Have you ever smelled a tannery? I had not. Which is to say that in the end we did not take the tour of the facility that we had never actually agreed to take. We peeped inside and saw men with stained hands holding poles and stalking the pools full of chemicals and skins. Some of them smiled at us. Nearby, you could buy finished leather products that had started in these pools. Well, of course they had started on the backs of subsequently flayed animals. We paid our final guide and left.

"The Approach to Al-Mu'tasim" predates the stories that would eventually come to surround it—first in *The Garden of Forking Paths* and then in *Ficciones*—by some years. In that sense it is an ur-story.

*Ficciones* is one of the first books I read when I was beginning to think of becoming a writer. I took it to Japan with me and read it carefully in the evenings. *Moby Dick,* which I am currently rereading, and *The Sound and the Fury* were other books I read carefully during that period. Or tried to.

I was much closer to my youth in those days. In my youth I read all the *Tarzan* books and all the *John Carter of Mars* books and all of *Elric of Melniboné.* In my youth, before I fell asleep, I liked to imagine I was some brave lieutenant in an impossible army. Also I was into Honda ATVs, their line of three-wheelers specifically, and had a teenaged obsessive's knowledge of their various makes and manufactures. Three-wheeler fantasies combine more fluidly with impossible armies than you might think.

Borges had a thing for circles, for reflections, for knife fights, and for mysteries. Borges was a big-time fan of G. K. Chesterton, whose stories I admire significantly less than he did.

Jack Spicer wrote a mystery novel. I read it but cannot remember whether it involved a murder or not.

I had the idea one night when I couldn't sleep at the riad in Marrakech that I needed to write a mystery in which the corpse at the center of the proceedings was a smartphone with a knife stuck through its screen. Combined with this was the idea that a man had come to believe he had been bewitched by his husband because said husband always knew how to make him smile. The man acted poorly when he came to this conclusion. But the bewitching didn't stop.

Be all that as it may, and regardless of my clear standing during much of the visit, I mean as a tourist—staying in riads, visiting tombs, being led to tanneries, and so forth—we were in Morocco by invitation to lay the groundwork for an artistic intervention at Half Moon. Half Moon was the site of a future community of luxury condominiums on Morocco's Atlantic coast.

If it is still there it is situated some forty kilometers south of Casablanca on the El Jadida road.

For some years after construction started and quickly stopped in the late 1990s, Half Moon was a kind of wasteland of potential, a kind of ruin in reverse. There was a brightly colored entrance gate and a guardhouse, a sloping stretch of flattened land. There was a multistory model building, never finished, standing

like a gray tooth sticking out of a stump of brown and green gums, like a tattooed fist punching up out of the earth,

like a ladder-faced stone giant's thumb.

There was also a long sheet of sandy soil leading down to a wide beach and then to the sea.

Eleni, Eva, and I, with our friends David, Celine, and Rebecca, went down from Casablanca to Half Moon in early June 2011. Construction on the site, David told us as we approached, had recently restarted, and it was true that as we passed through the entrance gates we could immediately see the early signs of it, excavators and other heavy equipment parked (we went on a Sunday) in the distance, newly graded protoroads cut through the sandy soil, enormous pieces of concrete piping scattered promisingly about.

Also everything looked dead and long abandoned. The way even an average construction site on an off day can.

The site, when it was completed, would still be called Half Moon.

Half Moon is both (what barely is and what will be).

It was (almost and not quite).

It is (never and nearly).

It would be (the main book I was reading during our trip was *Le Jardin des Plantes* by Claude Simon).

You know.

Maybe.

Whatever.

Right.

Borges was blind. He was not blind when he wrote "The Approach to Al-Mu'tasim," but he ended his days as a blind man. Milton was blind too. Ahab had his leg torn off by a whale and was blind to caring about the consequence of his ferocity.

Milton's Satan was heroic. Mine, if that is who it was, I mean in my dream, was some kind of a spy. He seemed to be a very good listener. He might well have been wearing a trench coat. I can't remember his eyes.

At Half Moon that day we were joined by the artist Hassan Darsi and his family, but not before having our car broken into. We were having a look at the beach and considering spots for our picnic when someone threw a large rock through the driver's-side window. When David and I returned to the car after being gone no more than ten minutes we found shattered glass. David and Celine's phones and papers and house keys (in the bag with the papers) were gone. Nothing else was taken. The picnic supplies were intact.

David was remarkably calm about the break-in. So was Celine.

From where we ate our lunch, Half Moon's model building could be seen.

We had bread and salad and some grilled chops and sausages.

Sand blowing into the food was a minor problem.

The grains weren't especially fine, but the wind. . . . the wind wasn't messing around.

A few days later, Eleni, Eva, and I took the train to Marrakech and had our adventure at the tanneries, then walked back to the Jemaa el-Fnaa, the great square at the city center where Barbary apes, orange juice stalls, snake charmers, traditional water vendors carrying brass cups, dancers, magicians, and storytellers abound. We bought the sorts of things tourists do (slippers, bags, scarves) in the souk and ate both our principal meals at the Terrasse des Epices, where Eva danced to Neil Diamond ("Sweet Caroline") and Karen Carpenter (I forget which song). During dinner we heard the evening call to prayer, the muezzins chanting from at least three nearby mosques.

Of course we heard the muezzins in Casablanca too.

We did not hear them at Half Moon. The wind and sea were too loud. We heard nothing.

Large plants with spiky leaves abound in that landscape. No one knew what the plants were called.

Driving into the site I saw a donkey in the distance. I have also seen donkeys in the distance in China, Greece, California, and France. I have seen donkeys in the distance in Corsica, Germany, England, and Canada. I can walk right up to a donkey and put a carrot in its mouth and it will still be a donkey at a distance to me. There is a hazy color to that distance. There is a shape, a texture, a weight, a blur.

Still and regardless, after lunch we decided to go and have a look at the model building. It sat next to an open cistern full of murky trash.

With the exception of Hassan, who had decided to walk back up to the gates—collecting plants, some of them the spiky ones, from the site as he went, he had been visiting Half Moon for years already, had made of film of himself jogging the site, his investigations of Casablanca are becoming the stuff of legend, probing its interstices, we visited his studio, saw his outrageously intricate scale model of the city amusement park, sold now to the Centre Pompidou in Paris, his gold leaf work, his videos, the view from his windows, all the staircases and wires and satellite dishes of Casablanca, etc.—all of us got out and poked around in the building. The unfinished floors were covered in sand and dirt. On the second floor we found some of David and Celine's things. The thieves must have run there to sort through their haul. Been in there while we milled about, while we set up our picnic site and fought the blowing sand. I took numerous pictures of the model building during our lunch, including some with a piece of mica I'd picked up in New Mexico partially covering the lens. It was easy to imagine afterward that the thieves had still been in there while I snapped away. Easy to see them standing there, staring at us from one of the windowless windows.

Mainly what we kept hoping to find were the house keys. Hassan's son Mansour had all kinds of interesting theories. He was quite the budding detective. One theory involved the cistern. I steadied him as he leaned out one of the windows to look at it. But we didn't. Find the keys I mean. The small girls were getting tired. It was hot. The picnic by the beach was over.

Half Moon was unfinished. So is this essay. I don't know what this essay is trying to say.

Still, we did not leave Casablanca without visiting le Marché aux Sorcières, where we saw tiny owls in cages eating the remains of their fellows and lovely piles of spices and dead coyotes hanging from ceiling beams. While the little girls had their hands and feet hennaed, I took a walk and saw men sitting on a piece of cloth in a circle playing brightly colored cards and betting bits of carrot. Elsewhere, there was a Monsieur de Charlus moment at the bar at the top of the Hotel Washington. The moment occasioned immense laughter. Also, we went for a drink at Rick's Café. This full-scale simulacrum, opened during the first decade of the twenty-first century, serves a nice cocktail. The four of us, Eleni, Laird, Celine, and David, sat at the bar. David was wearing pink jeans.

We had dinner later with Hassan at a fish restaurant near the water. There was a soccer match on the television. The restaurant was crowded. Bustling. Beautiful. Half Moon is a fist slowly uncurling its fingers. There we were. Wind off the water. Grilled meat and sand. The devil, carried over from America in the suitcase of my brain, leaned in closer. I asked David a few questions about Robert Pinget. The devil shook his head at my stupidity and we all got quite drunk.

# CLIMB THE WHALE

So. I wanted to write a Western set in the 1870s involving a gunhand who is contracted to kill an abusive father by a pair of brothers who then have a change of heart once the job is done and get up a posse to ride him down.

And then I wanted to write a Western that would end with a gunfight in waist-high snow.

And then I spent time considering whether these two ideas might not be parts of the same story.

And then I decided that maybe what I mainly wanted was to acquire for myself a fine new pair of jeans.

Not that jeans—which weren't widely distributed and affordable until well into the 1900s, so were little seen adorning the legs thick and thin of actual nineteenth-century gunfighters—are typically worn in Westerns. Indeed, I have long found it appealing that so much horse riding and six-gun shooting would be undertaken in slacks and vests and suits.

The association is indirect.

In high school I wore Levi's. Specifically, 501 button flies with the essential red rather than orange back-pocket tab. Most of my friends wore Levi's too. At some point, if we could afford it, we added Levi's jean jackets. Mainly we just stood around in this gear. Often in circles. It felt real. It was a thing. But an important percentage of my schoolmates favored boot-cut Wrangler jeans. The kids who wore these tended to sport big-buckled belts (we of the Levi's absolutely never did) and well-worn cowboy boots. They tended to have serious chores involving animals to do when they went home. And though central Indiana wasn't horse country, often the men these Wrangler-sporting schoolmates looked up to and in some cases would themselves go on to become were referred to as hands. The distance between hired hands and gunhands is not as great as you might think. In the case of certain cold-eyed weather-beaten individuals you might occasionally encounter at the feedstore or grain elevator the overlap is almost total.

Therefore, I took a trip over to the closet to see if I needed some new denim. Knowing full well then as now that needing and wanting are two different things. But I wasn't really sure, even as I went to the closet, that I was wanting, and thought maybe determining if I was needing would help me to better know.

In my closet, I found one pair of black jeans, one pair of gray jeans, and two pairs of blue jeans. In high school I would have considered the black and gray pairs, which are generously dosed with an elastic polymer, to be slacks, not jeans, but I have changed since then. Not long ago I had a pair of burgundy jeans, similar to the gray ones, but I gave them away in Athens along with a couple of shirts. Or rather I should say I left them, clean and neatly folded, on a bench on a square in the center of a neighborhood (Exarcheia) with a significant refugee population.

I did a lot in my button fly jeans in high school. I stood in those circles. I went around with my girlfriend. I leaned against lockers. I bantered with my teachers. I carried bags of groceries for my grandmother. I got into modest trouble. I rolled my eyes at the Wrangler wearers. They rolled their eyes at me. Probably we punched at each other a little too. Nothing serious. After all, we were all still brothers in jeans. There is a photo of me in my senior yearbook, taken after I badly injured my knee and had stopped, though I did not quite know it yet, being a serious athlete, in which I am leaning over a pair of crutches, wearing a dark-green football jersey and the 501s in question.

There were teachers I liked and teachers I didn't at that school. I had quite a few friends but these were not, as it turned out, and despite numerous weepy testimonials at graduation, friendships that would stand the test of time. And my girlfriend is long gone. There were tears there too. She married a farmer and had at least three kids, one of whom was a state-champion gymnast. My girlfriend was also an athlete of note. In her day. Years ago. Which of course was also my day.

I have never liked that expression.

And I don't know if the first time my girlfriend and I went past second base—on the gently sloping roof of her parents' garage, where we often went to talk and make out under the stars above Clinton County—I was wearing my button flies. I am fine not knowing this. It is not a detail that substantively obtains. We would never have arrived at that intimate juncture because of my jeans no matter what their brand or how good I imagined I looked in them. I don't know what my girlfriend was wearing that night either. Sweats possibly. She owned a pair of black parachute pants that fit magnificently. She drove a dark blue truck when she finally got her license. She liked to drive fast. She had this in common with my wife, Eleni. Eleni loves to lean on the accelerator. She is very often unsatisfied by the routes I choose and how gently I go. Go forward. Go along.

Here is the story involving a gunhand who got chased down for successfully doing a job by the people who had hired him. When they finally catch up after two days of hard pursuit in cold weather, he is drinking whisky at the counter of a bare-bones San Luis Valley saloon. It is wintertime in Colorado and cold. The chasers and the chased spend some time sizing each other up but also drinking whisky and coffee and talking, a lot of talking—it's an eclectic group—about life and the cosmos, and certain astronomical discoveries of note, the lesser-known works of Miguel de Cervantes, and the invention of submersible ships during the Civil War. When cards are brought out and the discussion grows involved, the gunhand takes the brothers aside and convinces them that since their change of heart has introduced an element of betrayal into the equation—one he gently but pointedly suggests the rest of the posse might be interested in knowing about—it wouldn't be right to just tie him up and drag him back to town. They should draw guns on each other out in the street. This way of settling things is not just something that happens in the dime novels, he says in reaction to an objection made by the younger brother. It is actually something that happens. His decent but not-excessive gun speed and reasonable but not-overwhelming accuracy would be deployed against their advantage in numbers. Numbers always beat speed and accuracy is his opinion on the matter, but he has never seen them shoot and is willing to take a chance.

The brothers are agreeable and no one from the posse raises any objection. They are all worn-out from the ride, and being in the warm saloon with drinks in their hands and many things to talk about has made them sleepy, and not even the second deputy sheriff in their number is overly concerned about the intricacies of formal justice. So the cards are put down and out the saloon doors they all go. And find a world transformed: while they were imbibing and sizing each other up and engaging in stimulating discourse, significant quantities of fresh snow fell. The snow was then piled high all along the thoroughfare by strong winds. When the three disputants are off the considerably raised sidewalks they discover that the snow comes up past their waists. All of them are glad that they took the time and expense to board their horses at the livery stable. A couple of tertiary posse members please themselves even as they consider the deep snow and contemplate the fight to come by imagining how relatively warm and well-fed their horses must be after the hard journey. The saloonkeeper has painted a pretty picture of the warmth and equine luxury of the stable. This comforts them. They look at each other and smile and wonder if they are smiling about the same thing and decide they are. One of them even remarks that he wishes he were a horse.

I am not sure whose point of view we would be in through all this. My first thought is the gunhand's, but maybe that wouldn't be so interesting. At least not at this moment. Maybe it would need to be one of the brothers, the older one I think, who has been having serious second thoughts about having first hired the gunhand and then turning on him for doing exactly what he and his younger brother, after all, paid him to. He is not a bad guy, this older brother, though at this juncture in his life he couldn't quite be called a good guy either. He is kind to his livestock and not unpleasant to his mother, who is home watching dry-eyed over the body of her dead tyrant husband.

The summer before, this brother engaged a miner he encountered outside Leadville on the subject of the unusual sturdy cloth his pants were made from. The miner told him he had gotten his pants when he was passing through Nevada. The pants were a little stiff but extremely durable, the miner said. The brother, and I offer this as a general comment on his preoccupations, would like someday to acquire a pair of his own. He even, in the moment, there in Leadville, with some squint to his eye, tried to determine if he and the miner were the same size. But they weren't. So the nefarious inclinations that sometimes overcame him during his early years weren't offered motivation to activate. He was glad about this.

Anyway, for obvious reasons the central parties (which is to say the two brothers versus the gunhand) have a hard time getting the showdown started. Their fingers are quickly frozen and their belt-holstered guns splay out sideways on the snow. More talking happens. The idea of shooting it out in the stables, the only building in town big enough to host such an event, is brought up, then rejected as being too disruptive to the animals, a quick decision that provides, for those whose thoughts had drifted over that way, considerable relief. Let the animals be. They are hard workers and deserve their rest. The saloonkeeper brings hot coffee out to the gunhand and whisky to the brothers. It is hard to determine which beverage would have the more salubrious effect in the situation. They debate this for a few minutes with the result that the two brothers wish they were drinking coffee instead of whisky and the gunhand wishes he were drinking whisky instead of coffee. And both sides verbalize this. The saloonkeeper then, with great understanding, brings all three of them mugs of coffee generously dosed with whisky, noting that, if they prefer, they can think of it the other way around. It crosses the older brother's mind as they are all out there in the snow, in their dusters and suits, that it might have been in some way advantageous, in addition to slurping on coffee with whisky, which tastes awful but feels good, to be wearing heavy blue cotton instead of thin, raggedy wool.

I myself have worn denim in the snow. I have done so in Indiana, New York, Holland, France, Colorado, Connecticut, and Rhode Island. The snow has often stuck in flat geometric clumps to the lower portion of my jeans. The geometric shapes have made me think of the work of certain abstract expressionists. Kazimir Malevich in particular comes to mind. When the geometric snow clumps have melted they have saturated the lower portion of my jeans, refreshing their variously deteriorated blues.

It is interesting to speculate on how the natural drying process affected the damp lower portion of my jeans once I removed and hung them, as was my habit, over an open door. No doubt if I had allowed them to dry on my legs a different process would have occurred. Of course I have for a very long time worn the sort of jeans that are so preconditioned—Sanforized is the proper term—that the interesting effects that enthusiasts of raw selvage denim seek to engender by never washing but occasionally wading out into rivers or jumping into swimming pools or sitting in bathtubs, then allowing them to dry without taking them off would not have been seen. My younger sister is something of an expert on real jeans, the kind whose fabric can be authentically sourced—now that the last shuttle looms have left the United States— only in Japan. She was kind enough recently to share some thoughts on warp and weft and selvage and slub and soaking and loom chatter and long wear and fade. She spoke of how wallets or phones, for example, carried always in the same place in the same pocket could create the interesting fades that help give a pair of jeans their unique personality.

This made me think of the lasting circular outlines created by tins of chewing tobacco carried in the back pockets of jeans in the 1980s of my youth. Chewing tobacco, or dip, like the 501s, was a whole thing at Clinton Central Junior-Senior High School, a thing I proved completely immune to when I tried it once in my teens and then again in college. I don't know how I might have reacted had I tried it later, during the years I was a smoker, when I was so well accustomed to nicotine, but the combination of buzzing and spitting and talking funny left me untempted. I wondered if I had continued to carry a comb in my back pocket, as I had done every day in eighth grade, when I still wore corduroys as often as I wore jeans, whether I might have ended up with an interesting and discussable comb fade, but the flatness of the instrument and its propensity to shift around in my pocket and the frequency with which I pulled it out to run it through my hair in the boys bathroom between and sometimes during class might have worked against this. By the time button fly shrink-to-fit Levi's had entered my life, I no longer carried a comb with me to school every day and the chunky watermelon-flavored Jolly Ranchers and tubes of ChapStick and wads of tissues and notes from my girlfriend moved around in my pockets far too much to leave any kind of a trace. Too much about our earthly endeavors is like this. Like a piece of soluble candy in a pocket.

Whatever that means, I recently searched high and low without any luck in an album of photographs by the great Juan Rulfo for someone wearing jeans. There were girls and women in dresses and boys and men in white cotton pants or in suits. With jeans on my mind I had pulled the album off the shelf where it had sat for too long because it is handsomely bound with an edging of deep blue cloth that was denim-like in its feel and visual aspect. The black-and-white photos of landscapes and cities and people in the album, which was given to me by Eleni, were as satisfying as I remembered them: the visual equivalent of extraordinary artisanal bread or one of Bach's cello suites or a Bessie Smith song. There was love in the mix of their making is what I might be saying. And death and sorrow and fear and hope. The human dispensation. The old bipedal endeavor. Tasks grand and grandiose and small. We carry bundles of wood. We beat drums. We dance in our fancy, beaded gowns. We gaze across rocky slopes and nigh-on boundless plains and carry about with us the memory of celestial bodies as we go. What a miracle to have lived all this time under heaven's festive lights. Aldebaran, Sirius, Canis Major, Alpha Centauri.

Rulfo's principal subjects, in his great novel *Pedro Páramo,* were death and lineage and the tired traveler's return. It might have been reflecting on these as I flipped through the album's pages that made me think of the little photo of a dead finback whale on a beach near Provincetown, Massachusetts, that I came across earlier this fall when I was perusing a book from the late nineteenth century on the history of that storied town. The whale in the photo has two men standing on top of it. One of them, it now makes me happy to think, is the older brother, lone survivor of the battle in the snow. The years have passed and he has made his way east and invested the proceeds from the sale of his now-late mother's—she died of an embolism—spread and livestock in the watery industries. He still thinks more often than he cares to of that night when the gunhand's Colt failed and both he and his brother put not the first but the second or third bullets they fired into him, of how after they had swum through the snow to reach him the gunhand's gun finally did its job and his brother slumped over as well. He lost two toes to frostbite that night, toes he still sometimes feels, and so is squatting to help his balance on the uneven surface of the whale. He is marveling at both the view and the smell of the carcass, which has nothing, yet, to do with putrefaction. It is a spectacular smell. The smell of a great aquatic adventure come unbelievably to its end. He is wondering if some of the smell will be communicated to his clothes, which include a pair of Levi's jeans he came by honestly and is now never separated from, imagines it will, and can't decide if the prospect pleases him or not. He doesn't much socialize beyond his generally successful business dealings and lives alone in nearby Wellfleet. He suffers frequently from night terrors. Sometimes when he wakes his father is standing over him and other times he is standing over his dead brother and the gunhand in the snow.

I can't decide whether he owns a dog. It seems like it might be an act of kindness to let there be a dog in his life. I think he is the kind of man who would appreciate the company of a dog. When he was younger, he would not have, but he has changed in important ways since he hired what we would now call a contract killer to do what he and his brother, for a wealth of reasons he will likely never untangle, simply could not. There is also a dog sitting on the whale in the photograph and so it might be his. As I say, I can't yet decide. And I'm not at all sure the story that has not been written needs me to make decisions like this. Or if when the extraordinary move is made to build special railcars and take the huge dead whale on tour as far away as Chicago, as the book I perused in Provincetown says happened, he somehow comes along.

It did not take much of an effort to find a photograph of László Krasznahorkai wearing jeans. In the photo he is seated outside at a café with his legs crossed on a metal chair with a green plastic back. He is wearing a dark blazer and, unmistakably, especially when you zoom in, black denim. He has a pen in one hand and the side of his bearded face in the other. This professional photo was taken in Germany in 1999, which means he is a decade removed from the original publication of *The Melancholy of Resistance,* though it will still be some years before its release, in English translation, in the United States. Given that the lavishly acclaimed film adaptation of the novel by Béla Tarr, *Werckmeister Harmonies,* is almost certainly already in production at the time of the photo, it is possible that Krasznahorkai has just thought or is about to think about the dead whale that lies at the center of his novel and Tarr's film, the whale that is the principal exhibit of a traveling circus that comes to a gloomy communist town. Maybe Krasznahorkai, who will not become famous in the so-called English-speaking world for this particular work, has just written the word *whale,* which is to say *bàlna,* on the pad of paper he has on his black jean–encased knee. Maybe he has just written it several times. I can of course write it down on the pad for him. There, I've done it: his black jeans, which may well be useful in resisting minor effects of the weather and everyday spills and in blocking chilly breezes, cannot bracket him off from my suppositions, no matter how intemperate or inconsequential they are. Photographs are staging grounds for great dreams.

Which one might reasonably infer from the photographs taken, over time, of people posed in front of a historical monument that a French archaeologist I know has been collecting for some years. In these photographs, anonymous individuals and groups of people of all stripes stand in front of the Parthenon. Eyes full and backs now bathed in the aura of the ages, they turned themselves to the camera, which even at the moment of the soft, confirming click, no matter who was opening and closing the shutter, was ambiguous in its aims: are we holding pictures of people standing before a monument or of a monument standing behind people or of something else entirely? Who knows what devices mean by what we make them for and make them do? This archaeologist, a specialist in Minoan civilization and the much-photographed ceremonial ruins at Delos, said little to me about his motivation for amassing a collection of photographs that stretch back into the nineteenth century, though he did note, as we walked back from dinner one night, that the people in them change in their aspect a good deal over time while the monument itself remains relatively unchanged. He is a frequenter of flea and antique markets and moves his mind over many things. As we walked that night, he also described his efforts to document the presence of the French army in Greece during the First World War, remarking, as he did so, on the young provincial peasants who suddenly found themselves so far from home. How many of them, I didn't think to ask, found a way to have their pictures taken in front of towering columns or crumbling theaters or half-buried sphinxes? Pictures that might be carried proudly in a pocket or sent to the other side of Europe to be placed on a mantelpiece in a Breton or Alsatian village? Would they have climbed on top of some of the monuments in question? Like the brother in the story I am apparently trying to tell? Can dead whales be counted as monuments? And, if so, as monuments to what?

I think the dog belongs to the other man in the photo of the dead finback whale on the Provincetown beach. I don't yet know anything about the other man except, now, that this dog belongs to him and not to the brother, who once, years ago, played his part in killing someone during a snowy gunfight in Colorado's San Luis Valley. That evening, after climbing back down the whale and limping across the beach and back into town, he thinks for a moment of the scar on the cheek of the young gunhand he and his brother killed. He thinks too of the dog that is not his, thinks of what it might be like to have a dog trotting alongside him during the day and sitting at his feet in the evening. The scar on the gunhand's cheek was not overlarge but it was noticeable and after he had been killed it seemed almost, out there in the snow, to be shining. It figures in the nightmares the brother has. Sometimes in the nightmares the scar is there and that is frightening and sometimes the scar is gone and that is frightening too. Most frightening of all though is when the scar appears on his own skin. On the back of his hand for example or on his ankle. Very rarely, the scar appears on his father. In place of his father's mouth. His father leans in close and whispers to him through the scar or presses the scar to the brother's brow or cheek. His jeans offer him no protection in this regard. He wonders if a dog might. The dog could sleep at the foot of his bed. Having a dog sleep in a bedroom in the 1880s in America is far from unheard of. It occurs to him that night, when he is in his bed in Wellfleet, that the presence of the dog might offer him protection, on the inside, the way his jeans offer him protection on the outside. He turns this over in his mind. He turns his body and his mind turns and the dog turns. On one of the turnings the hypothetical dog becomes the remembered dead whale. He stops turning. The dead whale now lies at the foot of his bed in the dark. It has crushed the bottom of his bed frame. It has blotted out the world of his house and the night beyond. It is curved in such a way that one of its great eyes looks at him. The rest of the whale is dead but the eye is not. Sometimes the eye blinks. When he turns again the whale is gone and the dog at the foot of his bed is a dead dog. Crushed by the whale. This dead dog does not offer him any protection. He is glad that at least he is trying to sleep, as he often does, in his jeans. He thinks more highly of them than I do of Krasznahorkai's. He thinks they can keep the eyes and schemes of other dreamers away. And it may be true that sturdy denim, *true* denim, of the kind my younger sister favors, that is made now mostly on special looms in Japan, has qualities that defy easy articulation.

Be that as it may, over the coming days, the brother watches as the whale gets loaded onto the specially built railcars. To be exhibited for as long as it lasts in the great interior of the giant country he has already seen so much of. Once upon a time it would have been a task almost past imagining to lift a whale and load it on a train but that time, even in the 1880s, is long gone. In respect of his investment, the brother is offered a place in the small entourage that travels with the whale but at the last minute declines. The man with the not-hypothetical dog goes instead. I do not know if he takes his dog with him. Or if the dog stays behind. Everyone during the leave-taking has the word *whale* in their minds and on their lips. Nineteenth-century Provincetown is a village of immigrants and they think it and say it in different languages: *hval, kit, cá voi, banginis, baleine, balena, walvis,* クジラ, *baleia, bálna.* Away the whale goes. America has always been and ever will be a republic of beautiful words.

And of terrible ruin. While the dead whale goes west through the ancestral lands of the Nauset, Wampanoag, Massachusett, Narragansett, and Nipmuc peoples, the buffalo are being slaughtered by the millions on the oceanic plains. Those that might have stood in meaningful numbers to defend them have been murdered or isolated or chased away. Land is being fenced off, interrupting natural migration and hunting patterns. The assault on groundwater is beginning in earnest. Ever-larger dams are being contemplated as rivers dry up. Holes are being cut through mountains. Entire forests are being chopped down. Treaties are being signed and broken. Often they are broken before they are signed. In many places slavery seems over in name only. Guns are being pointed in every direction at every second, which seems, to many, a thing to be inordinately happy about. Yes, guns and gunfights are far from over as the whale is rolled away, in fact one might say they are just getting started, and despite the good thoughts of their owners, some of the horses that sat snug in the barn during the snowy gun battle of yore were soon after ridden to death or to death's next door. One, for example, broke its leg in high snow and had to be shot in the head the very next morning. Its name was Helios. Its owner, the second deputy sheriff, was sad and inconvenienced in unequal measure and, because everyone else had already gone, taking the two now-redundant horses with them, had to wait for the better part of two months for a stage to come through town. He was not sorry his job was not waiting for him when he got home to Taos. Although he did not take part in the gunfight, he never fully got over the experience and ever after went about his affairs with a wary look in his eye.

As one might if one were required to negotiate a forest that had grown up almost overnight in a place where there were no woods before. If one were taken, say, in through the gates of a soccer stadium, blindfolded, led down the steps and out onto the pitch, only to discover, once the blindfold was removed, that one had been led into a woods like the one installed by the curator Klaus Littmann in the Wörthersee Stadium in Klagenfurt, Austria. An exhibit meant to raise awareness around issues of conservation, and that was met by howls from certain right-wing constituencies, but that makes me think more immediately of Maurice Sendak's *Where the Wild Things Are* or tales about lost children and their encounters with witches and wolves and sudden blizzards and lonely towers and giant fish.

Fairy tales happen all around us. They happened in the past and they will happen in the future and they are happening right now. Nearby. Look closely. Listen. Climb the whale. You might notice a strange smell. Don't be scared. Or not too scared.

When he is old, in the years just before World War One, a conflict that will see so many young people sent to places that push past easy imagining, the brother gets on a ship he is the principal shareholder of and takes the old whale road to Norway, the land where his father was raised. Upon arrival, walking with a cane, he visits the house where his father took his first breaths and emitted his first angry cries. He visits the church where his father bowed his little then not-little head. He visits the schoolhouse where, according to a tale once oft told, his father was regularly whipped and abused by some great brute named Master Pedersen, a monster whom his father would often evoke when he was caning and more than once breaking the bones of the two brothers for the slightest infractions. "Let's see if we can make Master Pedersen proud!" his father would shout before beating them until the bloody drops began to fly. Once when the father shouted this, the brother who died during the gunfight and has figured even less in this account than the gunhand shit his pants.

Everyone is very nice in the village. Very welcoming. He has first and second cousins there. One of them owns an inn where he takes a room. He speaks a little Norwegian and they compliment him and fuss over him. It is clear that he has money, that he has prospered, but the cousins don't seem overly interested in this and that pleases him. The rest of the village is not so discreet. Even though he is old now, girls are pushed forward to accompany him on his daily walks, which he is amused by as he has always nourished a preference for both the casual and the intimate company of men. After a few days, the mayor of the little village, who is not related to him, announces a feast in his honor. Fishermen have brought in a rare delicacy, the flesh of a Greenland shark. After it has been properly treated to mitigate its toxicity, the flesh is cooked into a pungent stew that the brother is only able to choke down out of politeness.

During the long meal he makes inquiries about Master Pedersen. No one can recall such a person. The current schoolmaster, Helberg, is called over. He says without hesitation that there has never been a Master Pedersen at the local school. He says there was a Master Bakker, a Master Olsen, a Master Amdahl, a Master Stensruhd, and a Mistress Bjørnsdotter, among others, but no Master Pedersen. Not in the past 125 years. He knows this because he has been contemplating writing up a history of the school and has already begun his research. When the brother lowers his voice and adds details that make his lip quiver to articulate, Master Helberg shakes his head again and says that while corporal punishment has never been anomalous in the area—and has its place even in his own classroom, he adds with a laugh and a swish of an imaginary cane—there was never a great brute named Pedersen who held the chalk and the cane. Perhaps the honored guest has the name wrong? After Master Helberg has excused himself the brother slumps back in his chair. He has of course made other inquiries, not just about Master Pedersen but about his father's now-long-dead parents and dead siblings but has uncovered nothing that might reasonably serve as the prime mover for the tale he has been telling himself for more than half a century. He knows there are many possible explanations and also that it is possible there are none.

He spends the night vomiting, then in the morning goes with a trio of girls—who are not interesting to him in the way the villagers might hope for them to be but are pleasant company nonetheless—to the church and lights a candle in memory of his awful father. As he lights it he bows his head and tells the candle, as a proxy for his father, that regardless of what did or didn't happen to his father when he was a boy and young man in this village, he wishes he had had the courage to shoot the bastard himself all those years ago. There had been no reason for such an elaborate plot. One that had resulted in three deaths. Instead of just one.

Thinking of elaborate plots, he turns away from the candle and tells the girls about the whale he chose not to accompany on its journey across America. He says he was tempted but that the mere idea of retracing his steps, even imperfectly and partially, had given him nightmares for weeks. He tells them that in the wake of those nightmares he often wondered if a creature as large as a whale took a much longer time to die than one might think. That whales died on the outside and could no longer move, but only slowly, layer by layer, perhaps over years, died on the inside, with their earliest memories slipping away last of all.

He tells them as they stand in the church beside the candle he has lit for the father he wishes he had been the one to shoot that he has sometimes, in the intervening years, imagined that the incompletely dead whale could feel him standing on top of him on the beach in Provincetown and that the whale carried that feeling of weight, his weight, along with it as it went west.

He says, "I jumped up and down on it. Can you imagine that? Jumping up and down on a possibly not fully dead whale. It was a strange sensation. Somehow I could do it without falling over. Even though I lost my two little piggies in the snow. I was squatting, then I stood up and just started jumping. With each jump an image came to me of the cottonwood trees of my boyhood. When they would lose their leaves the cottonwoods resembled images I used to enjoy looking at, of the inside of the brain and the path of comets and the fingers of large skeletons. When I landed on the deep rubber of the whale I saw stars and these stars looked like cottonwoods in winter to me is what I am saying, girls. There was a dog there too and it barked when I jumped up and down. Who knows what it thought of when I leapt. Several times I almost fell. The dog's owner was an ignoramus who worked for me. He laughed and spat tobacco onto the whale and thought his own vulgar thoughts. I did not like that and stopped jumping up and down. I was wearing jeans."

"Jeans?" says one of the three girls, the only one who has a little English. She is very interesting looking, the brother thinks. All three of them are. He tries to picture them in jeans. Sees them for a moment clad in stiff blue cloth and jumping up and down on the whale. Their names are Birgit, Ingrid, and Lotte. Birgit plays the cello. Ingrid loves reading and writing stories set in outer space. Lotte, the one who recognized the word "jeans," is a very good dancer and is into shoplifting. He will learn all about this later. In the days to come. In the meantime, he has not worn jeans in years but can vividly remember the comforting pressure they applied to his legs and wishes he had a pair he could put on.

"I shot a man once," he says, making his hand into a pistol and firing off a few loud rounds right there in the church, so that the girls, whose names he does not yet know, laugh politely but also look nervously at the altar and even, though it is not at all their custom, surreptitiously cross themselves. "In the snow," he says, blowing imaginary smoke off the end of his finger while with the other hand he mimes gently falling flakes. The girls think he is now telling a story about a butterfly or a bird that has fallen out of its nest or a gentle autumn rain of the variety that will be falling soon. The story he wants to try to tell though, which was brought back to him by the signs of the cross being made, is about how, as a boy in northern New Mexico, he overheard a priest in one of the churches his father wouldn't attend but liked to visit at off-hours, often with his unhappy sons in tow, explain that the holes in Christ's hands were the place where stories came from. He holds up both his cupped hands to the girls and they think he is hungry and begin to speak amongst themselves about what food they might bring to him or bring him to but what he is asking them is what they see in the center of his palms. "I see a whale in one and a snowstorm in the other," he says. He asks them what they see in the center of their own palms and for a few moments they all stand there with cupped hands outstretched in the uncertain light of the candle he has lit for his father, then he laughs and leaves them and limps back out into the sun.

For one reason or another, the earlier-mentioned high-school girlfriend and I played a good deal of "guess which hand." By that I mean one or the other of us would hold out both hands, closed tight over something tempting, and ask the other to guess where it was. Inside the winning hand would be some Red Hots or a piece of Starburst or a Tootsie Roll or a love note. Speaking of which, once, when I was walking past her in school and she was at her locker and I was preparing to scare her she spun around at the last minute and had me guess a hand. The first one looked empty and so did the second.

"I'm holding the note you didn't write me but should have," she said.

"Here's my note," I said without missing a beat, and right there in the middle of the hallway I kissed the center of one of her pretty, empty palms and then the other. And then I walked on, almost certainly wearing my 501s, and my girlfriend watched me walk, and as I went she gave out a low, slow whistle. And though I didn't know it then I know it now that what had just unfolded between us was a story entire. One whose details may wobble but will never finish being told.

"Once recorded, a story has the potential to live longer and spread farther than any other creature. All it requires is a consciousness to inhabit—and that consciousness need not be human or even organic," writes Ferris Jabr in an essay called "The Story of Storytelling," which describes the almost inconceivably deep and interconnected origins of the tales found in the Grimms, in Andersen, and in Perrault, and their counterparts on other continents. Stories, like fire—that special, manageable fire that was stolen from the gods—have really never stopped spreading, and if it is true that some portion of them that we now tell has passed through the bloody holes in the hands of a Jewish carpenter pulled down off a Roman cross two thousand years ago, they are much, much older than that.

Some are so old they can barely move.

A bit of black bark with an eye at its center. A warm dollop of weeping dough.

Some are just in the opening act of becoming ancient.

Say an upturned empty hand held out in a Norwegian church. Or in the hallway of an Indiana high school.

What do you see at the center of your empty hands? When you hold them out in front of you. Forests? Snowstorms? Bonfires? Deep pools? The fade—think raw denim—from a kiss you had forgotten you had been given in your own personal long ago? The fade from a wound that for better or worse means a great deal to you?

These are among the sorts of things that can be hard to determine. That gnaw at us as we gnaw at them.

What I am able to determine at this moment is that since I read on Wikipedia that they can live for more than four hundred years and that they have been found with all kinds of land animals in their guts and that they are one of the very largest sharks, and that over the centuries, as copepods attach themselves to their corneas, they go completely blind, down there in the dark waters they favor, and that they are often to be found in the deepest parts of the ocean and have toxic flesh, the Greenland shark gets my vote for most frightening undersea entity.

I'm not sure, despite his having eaten part of one the night before, if the brother is thinking about Greenland sharks that afternoon when, having made his apologies to the girls, and naked as the day he was born, he swims out into the cold though not intolerable waters that lap along the low beach near his father's village. But probably he should be. Several besides the one that was caught have been spotted in the environs. What I know for certain is that, having mentioned jeans earlier in the church, he is thinking about the last pair he owned. That he still owns though they are far away. He wore them every day in the years before it became more appropriate for him to wear suits with waistcoats. Over time during those years the warehouse key he kept in his front left pocket created a fade that lingered long after he sold the warehouse and surrendered the key. He left the pair of jeans, unworn now for a great while, neatly folded in a drawer in the large Wellfleet house I feel ever more certain he will never return to. The shape of the fade in

those folded jeans is approximate. Someone else looking at them, perhaps someone disposing of his posses-
sions after his death, might not know what caused it. But
he knows. He has scars on his back and he knows what
caused those too. He is thinking that if he had already
had jeans to wear when he was young, that if he and
the miner had been the same size, and he had worked
up enough courage to steal them, he might have felt just
buffered enough by the thickness and stiffness of the fabric not to agree to his brother's suggestion that they hire
the gunhand who had just ridden into town. He might
have felt that he could withstand what had largely become
the verbal blows handed out by his father now that he
and his brother were as big as he was. It doesn't concern
him, as he swims over the cold dark waters, that the protection of jeans, like the comfort of dogs, has never in
his experience been more than notional: something, he
thinks, is gargantuanly better than nothing. It's the story
of the universe. The oldest one there is. He wishes he
had thought of this in the church so that he could have
said something about it to the three girls.

Wishing this makes it all the more remarkable that
when he turns around to head back to shore (this has not
despite the likely proximity of Greenland sharks been
either a death or slow-fade swim) he sees that Birgit,
Ingrid, and Lotte, never mind that he still doesn't know
their names, are waiting for him on the beach. They
stand shoulder to shoulder in a smart Scandinavian
line. Birgit holds his shoes, Ingrid his clothes, and Lotte,
he is happy to see, what looks like a towel. Their other
hands are cupped and outstretched. Most tantalizingly.

When, however, he has climbed out of the water and begun to approach, they one after the other close them. Whereby he thinks again of the notable fade in his jeans in Wellfleet, which looks to him now, in his mind's eye, not so much like a key but like the shape of the look he and his brother exchanged while the gunhand was putting his proposition to them in the San Luis Valley saloon. The look comes to him now from across the years. By doing this we can atone, the look said. But atone for what? the look also said. For not killing him ourselves, the look said. But we would never have done it, the look said. This is true but still, the look said. He is dead, the look said. Mort, morto, tot, νεκρός, smrt, dood, marbh, marw, nie żyje, halott, hildako, dead.

When he reaches the girls, he first takes the towel and dries himself off. He is not embarrassed to be naked. He is far too old for that. The decades have stripped him of his vanity. In fact he never had much vanity to begin with. He takes his clothes and puts them on and then takes his shoes and puts them on too. All the while the girls stand with their closed hands outstretched. "Choose," says Birgit. All three of them have large hands. He looks carefully at their long, closed fingers. He is hoping that in the center of the hand he chooses he will find a tiny pistol and pair of jeans.

Recently, while I was wearing the new jeans that I did buy at the start of this essay, I stumbled across a photograph of a vertically aligned whale sleeping underwater with her vertically aligned calf sleeping underwater next to her. Around the same time I came across a photograph of a

392-year-old Greenland shark swimming upward, alone and at an angle, through the dark. I don't know how what started as whales ended up as sharks but sometimes it's just like that.

These are all the sorts of things that can be seen in the fades of one's jeans if one has a mind to.

For the fades of one's jeans are associated with the folds in one's mind.

Which I can write here. But that does not make it true.

# THIS WIDE TERRAQUEOUS WORLD

Then it was time to leave so I said goodbye to the dead
cats buried in the backyard and left them with a toy
and a little of the sliced turkey they had always loved and
looked at the yard where we had planted so many things
and eaten so many meals and set up hammocks and cro-
quet courses and tents and inflatable pools all devoured
by the years now of course and walked out the front door
of the empty house. I took a picture of myself with the
1180 number plate by the front door and texted the picture to Eva and Eleni. The number plate was not a thing
of great beauty. In fact I had always entertained thoughts
of replacing it. There were purple flowers blooming
in the beds. The side yard looked sweet and tidy. The
peaks we could see above the neighbors' houses across
the street were tall, cragged, and handsome as they
always would be. There was a light breeze in the leaves
of the silver maple. Somewhere down the street someone was mowing. I thought of the green lawnmower we
were leaving behind. It was not a fine lawnmower though
the orange extension cord that we used with it was all
but new. I made sure the plants I was transporting
were well secured and that the liquor bottles from our

emptied cabinet couldn't be seen from outside the car and wouldn't rattle too much when I drove. It was a fine day, but I'd heard there was weather coming up in the evening and wanted to get out ahead of it. Eleni and Eva were already in Providence. With the cats that weren't dead. Our old friend Reed had taken them to the airport the day before while I oversaw the final stages of the packing and loading and signed the necessary forms.

I backed out of our driveway one last time, rolled down Edinboro, which I had always had to spell for people and now wouldn't anymore, curved around on Yale, turned right on Table Mesa, and made for the highway. As always, there were people in snug bike gear. Some of them looked quite fit. I drove south and east to Denver, past the glimmering, fizzing refinery that had always reminded me of a story by Richard Ford whose name I can't remember and probably won't hunt for and over the Platte. The Platte looked a little sad, kind of beat up. I had always had mixed feelings about it. I did not get to see it during the floods of 2013 because we were in Cleveland for an award ceremony. It would have looked much different during that 100-year event. I stayed on US-36 instead of jumping onto I-70. The bottles did not rattle and the plants seemed to be doing fine though the Norfolk pine was chafing the back of my arm so I gently draped a dish towel over it.

Soon, the mountains vanished from sight. The road was straight and, after that rise out of Boulder, mostly flat and there were many black cows in the fields. I played music and started listening to some audiobooks. At first I couldn't get my phone to connect to the car speakers so I tucked it up into the visor near my head. I had a choice between Tolkien and a Japanese novel about a woman who enjoys working in a convenience store. I made my first stop in Cope, Colorado, to stretch my legs and take a few pictures of tumbledown buildings. I like tumbledown buildings. The town name was neatly decaled onto an old oil barrel. I saw a bloated, ant-nibbled cat by the side of the car and of course thought of the cats we had left buried in the backyard.

Idalia and St. Francis went by too quickly with their beautiful names and marvelous grain silos that rose up out of the flatlands like battle towers in *Star Wars* or Jodorowsky's vision of *Dune*. The Tolkien book—an excerpt from *The Silmarillion,* which I read many times as a boy and once as a young man—was narrated by Christopher Lee. An hour later I stopped in McDonald, which had a small park next to the road. There were bright blue trash barrels and a hexagonal white merry-go-round. Most merry-go-rounds have been yanked up out of the American earth, but clearly in places like McDonald, Kansas, they had been allowed to live on. I did not get on the merry-go-round as I once would have, perhaps even not that long ago, but I did make it spin and took little videos. Off in the distance, on the other side of the road, beyond a derelict yellow school bus, a watering contraption gave the impression of some monstrous metal grasshopper preparing to leap. The pictures I took of it with my phone were not satisfying. It is possible I took one with my good camera, an Olympus, but that remains to be confirmed.

That night I watched most of a John Wayne movie about robbing an armored stagecoach and drank a can of Bushido-brand sake in an Econo Lodge in Phillipsburg, Kansas. The can was small and black with red highlights and sported a white fox with a topknot and a pair of swords. I tested the Geiger counter I had ordered for the trip. The numbers told me little. The South Asian woman on night duty who had checked me in was very pleasant. I had snack-type things for dinner. The room was very clean. It rained a great deal during the night and when I went out to check on the car, whose contents I hadn't quite had the courage to fully empty, I met a muscular young man smoking a cigarette next to a muscular rottweiler. I smiled at the young man and he did not smile back but did not seem unfriendly.

Early the next morning when I went out the rain had stopped and I met an older woman with hair that would have been eye-poppingly large even in the 1980s. She too had a dog with her. It seems improbable now but I think it was a mastiff. I loaded up. The pastries on offer in the lobby did not seem appealing so I abstained. If the woman from the previous night had been there I might have taken one and even given it a chomp in her presence but she was not there. I cannot remember who was. I found a café in downtown Phillipsburg and waited a very long time for what turned out to be one of those '90s-style cappuccinos that came with nutmeg and cinnamon and were much too weak. Was there a moment when writers made fun of the amount of time it can take to make certain kinds of large espresso drinks in small midwestern towns? I feel like there may have been. That is not my intent here. There was a lot of candy for sale in the café. Giant lollipops and taffy and bags of caramel corn. Everyone seemed happy in ways that could not just be explained by the sweet stuff. Happy and a little worn out. Like certain characters that pop up at the edges of Lucia Berlin stories. Lucia is not pronounced *Lu-sha*. Nor is it pronounced *Lu-chee-ah*. I know this because I knew her a little. In the short course I took with her we read Chekhov and *Loving* by Henry Green. Lucia was very kind to us and generous with her knowledge.

The blueberry scone I purchased to go with my cappuccino was better than I expected it would be, but I did not eat it quickly. I drove off under blue sky and huge clouds. Everything looked drenched and fresh. The air in the car felt like cool sheets. Likely I was a little underslept. There was no need to turn the air conditioner on. As I drove, I thought a little of the people I had seen in the café, smiling and talking and touching each other's forearms. I had not felt happy the previous day, the day of departure, when I was racing away from all we had left behind in my attempt to beat the weather, and worrying about the plants and the bottles and the boxes of photos and treasures from Eva's early days, but I did then as I drove east into the huge, clearing clouds, then turned north on Highway 281 and started to think about my impending morning visit, not too many miles up the road, to the onetime home of Willa Cather in Red Cloud, Nebraska.

Are people still reading Willa Cather? I remember Paul Auster asking that question some years ago, if somewhat rhetorically, about André Gide. I mean, as I think he meant it, *reading* Willa Cather. In typing that, and thinking about some of her short stories set deep in the marrow of Nebraska, and about some of her novels that seem so beautifully drunk on the deeper notes of life's best natural beauties, I register that I have sometimes wished that we had finer gradations of typographical emphasis, ones that went beyond and between standard boldface and italics and strikethroughs, so that we didn't have to resort to the cutesy imagery of emojis, which the culture has embraced, for the duration I fear, so underlinedly. Willa Cather's *Death Comes for the Archbishop* is one of the finest books set in the West I know, and I have read a few. I had it more in mind than *My Ántonia*—though I love that one too and it takes place in something much like the bulged and creek-cut cropland I had all around me—when off on a rise a mile or so from 281 I saw an abandoned house it took my fancy to get a picture of. So down a gravel road I gaily went. Only the gravel, in a betrayal I wonder if only fellow midwesterners will fully understand, vanished three-quarters of the way down, and when I turned right at the bottom, I just had time to say "oh-oh" and did say "oh-oh" and the car, which had been struggling, slid sharply left and slammed, stuck, into the grass bank the abandoned house sat behind.

My desire, it should be said, to take a picture of that abandoned house, a picture my mishap had the happy side effect of giving me plenty of time to snap, was in large part motivated by the impending publication of a small novel I had written about witches who don't want to be called witches but get called witches anyway. They all take a turn living in an abandoned house, decorated back into apparently pleasant being by the ruddy force of their memories and their desires, deep in a woods. As part of the publicity effort for that publication, which all knew was going to be a modest affair even if we held out hope for some pop anyway, I had agreed to put personal photos up on my publisher's Instagram account. Even though we were four hundred years and seventeen hundred miles away from the putative New England setting of my tale, this blank-windowed north Kansas farmhouse set on a slight eminence above a field it had long since been metabolized by seemed, in that context, promising.

There was no one around. The fields surrounding me were loud with insects and alive with birds. My shoes quickly became covered with mud. I walked north up the road for three-quarters of a mile and, though I'd gained elevation, could still see no houses or signs of life. I mean there were signs of life, of course, everywhere, in and on and above the muddy road whose quick-drying clods had now become a part of my Adidas, just not signs of life that might help me get my car out. This remained the case even when sometime later I did find a house—complete with pit bulls in a chain-link pen attached to the front of the house and parked red truck with a scoped rifle stored above the back seat—and knocked and knocked to the chorus of barking dogs, some of which were clearly now inside and just behind the door, and finally roused a woman. She told me that no, she didn't know anyone who could help me, and that I should call the police based in Lebanon, a town I had passed five miles back, but no, she didn't have a phone I could use, or the desire to place the call herself while I waited outside. Fair enough. I thanked her, went back to the car, got some water, locked it, scribbled a sign to put on the windshield, and walked a muddy mile out to the main road to try to find some kind of a signal.

The young man who arrived to help me, two hours later, had driven over from Phillipsburg, where I had started my day. There had been no trees out near the turnoff where I was to meet him so I had spent a good part of the time sitting in a ditch next to a bean field with a jacket over my head. That a light sunburn in a landscape that was pleasantly reminiscent of the rural Indiana environs I knew so well was all the weathering the episode had offered—when for someone who looked a little less like me it might well have been much more serious, perhaps even grave—was not lost on me. In fact it seemed then, and even more so now as I reflect, a fatal flaw not in the truth quotient of this story, if that is what it is, but in its worthiness for telling. Does my relative ease in this unfolding situation mark it as unworthy for recounting? I thought then and think now. Quite possibly. I mean, why tell it at all? Why tell anything?

Nevertheless, the mud had dried a good deal and as it turned out all I needed was a good push, which the young man was happy to offer. Once I was up the hill I stopped the car and paid him his money. I asked him if he would follow me until I was back on the main road just in case. I felt exceptionally grateful and definitely embarrassed as one does in these situations. He took the whole thing very seriously and said nothing about the plants in the car or about the car itself, which was and is a sky-blue Toyota Prius *v*. I had not seen any other hybrids that morning and did not see any after I waved to the young man and turned north and ran fast up to Red Cloud. For the first few yards on solid asphalt the mud flew off my tires with a wonderful, deep, whirring, rushing hum that quickly resolved itself into a sleety flickering and then nothing, beyond the sound of road and rubber, at all.

Red Cloud, which had not been expecting me, was in no way impressed by my tardiness. When, after I had spent a few minutes inspecting the Cather house, I visited the National Willa Cather Center and tried to talk a little about my travails, the woman who worked there took almost no notice of my speech act at all. So resolute was she in her posture of not listening that I began to suspect there was an invisible force field around her head, one that let her see out but that did not let sound, when she did not want it to, come in. This unsatisfactory—it really was quite invisible, even when I squinted my eyes and none too surreptitiously cocked my head—noise-cancelling force field hypothesis led me after a moment, during which I was still engaged in my speech act, to think of the Chris Nolan film *Interstellar,* in which a time-bending black hole plays an important role, and though nothing in the woman's expression or bodily gestures might indicate this, I started to imagine that just behind the door of her face was the entrance to a silently howling singularity, one she could crack open slightly to suck in and dispose of unwanted sound, perhaps by a clenching of her jaw or a slight lifting of her eyebrow, at the bottom of which, if it could be said to have a bottom, her heart was nonetheless still at work. She had papers in front of her. These papers required consulting. I was still standing there. I made, in conclusion of my speech act, a comment about how nice and cool it was in the museum, took a step backward, pivoted the way I had been taught many years before when I was a role-playing basketball player on a decent Indiana varsity basketball team, and stepped smartly toward the exhibits.

I went by the display cases at a speed that might euphemistically be called unnecessary. The floor creaked under my agitated feet. I tried to slow down. There were things that interested me. I am by nature interested in the Nachlass, in that which is left behind, and the strange things, like little museums housed in former small-town opera venues, that grow out of it. Nonetheless, I was overly aware of my sunburned face and neck. My scalp itched a little as if something small and mobile might have found its way down into its oils and folds. There were first-edition copies of books I loved and others I was interested in under glass, and bits of information that were new to me though I no longer remember much about them. How does one both represent and celebrate a life? One marked by curious circumstance. After all, Willa Cather, poet of the Nebraska prairie, had spent a hell of a lot of her time in Manhattan. Being in possession of this knowledge pleased me. Recently I went to the Jefferson Market Library in New York and discovered that they had a Willa Cather Reading Room. Willa Cather wasn't even born in Nebraska. That decisive event took place in Frederick County, Virginia. There were buttons to press. I mean there in Red Cloud. Like many I suppose, I have always liked to press buttons in museums but the truth is this time it was no good. I was still out there on the road with my car stuck and was furious with myself for having let it happen because I was on a schedule and Eleni and Eva and our two not-dead cats were expecting me. I was still walking up the driveway and still wondering if the dogs would stop barking and if anyone would answer the door. If the police came and cared to look a little closely at my affairs they would find that I had open whisky and mezcal and more than one variety of Greek liquor with me. I also had a certain number of delivery devices that contained THC. What were the Kansas road rules? I couldn't decide if the police would find all the plants suspicious or charming. I was still out on the main road waiting for my ride. It was hot but I had plenty of water. There was nothing wrong. Not really. It's important not to grow timorous if you don't have to. An older couple drove up and stopped their car. I was both embarrassed and grateful for their attention. They wanted to know if there was anything they could do to help. I told them what had happened and the man said he sure wished he had some chains and a hitch on his car. It was one of those big American soft-suspension jobs, a year or three into its service. I think it was deep burgundy in color but I may be confusing it with the Jeep Grand Cherokee, a gift from my aunt, that we drove for several years. I didn't take good notes on the trip. I told them that I had someone coming, that everything was all right. I am quite skilled at seeming all right. They smiled at my all rightness and we said a few more things about time and the weather then they drove on.

Bored of waiting—and because I wanted to find the starting point of a long line of leaf-cutter ants, normally not indicated in those environs, who were disappearing with their precious chips of green into the cornfield that led to the abandoned house—I set out walking. But not before I stopped back by the car and took out the bottle of single malt for encouragement and the Norfolk pine for company. It was scratchy, as I've already said, but fit reasonably well under one arm. Careful not to step on any of the ants, I struck out across the fields that would have once been prairies for Willa Cather to be pleased about. I have already said it was hot but the heat hits differently when you have whisky to consume and unlooked-for ants to watch and it is no longer about your car being stuck and wondering if anyone will ever show up to help. I walked through beans and corn. There were ditches to be traversed. The ground was necessarily muddy. Whenever I stumbled—as the ants never seemed to—the Norfolk pine brushed unlanguorously against my face but I did not let this trouble me. I had Johnny Cash's version of "Hurt" stuck in my head. My head was making it cheerier than Cash intended. My head put more of an accent on it. Probably I had been affected in this regard by the accents of the old couple who had wished they could help me but hadn't been able to. Before long the bottle of Laphroaig 10-Year-Old was empty. It had been a gift to us from the father of Eva's best friend. She and this friend had been close since sixth grade. The night of their parting they had both sobbed. The sobbing went on for many minutes. They rolled around on the ground together as Eva's best friend's stepfather and I looked on. Probably Eva, there in Providence, was either thinking about her best friend or speaking to her via FaceTime.

Every now and again my phone would get service but I could not think of anyone I needed to call. Or who needed me to call. I hoped my car was all right and that the man coming to help me would find it. I was going in one direction and the ants in another. There were many abandoned houses off in the distance. Grain bins and silos and farm implements towered all around.

When I was back on 36, walking on the shoulder, trying not to get hit by cars that weren't stuck, occasionally passing swaths of dead ants who had not been so lucky, I got it in my mind that, with another book around the corner, I should do some thinking about the years I had spent writing and the works that I had produced. There were the city books and the rural books. The books set in a present that was fast becoming past and the books set in a past that was skidding farther away. The books set in the present felt like they were growing staler by the second whereas the books set in the past felt relatively fresh. No doubt this was because it was all already long over for them. For what they were about. Their content. Their subject matter. Their information. Which I know—I've read my Benjamin—is the least interesting aspect, but still. . . . In the Peter Jackson film *They Shall Not Grow Old,* in which the past's silence has been given sound and its grays and sepias color, there is a scene in which one of the thusly resurrected soldiers, marching past huge slabs of rubble, aware of the camera pointed at him, repeatedly taps another soldier on the helmet with a pole. While most of the frame is indeterminate gray or washed-out brown, there is a shrub screen left and a tree screen right that are green. And there is the sound, also given to us by Jackson, of the pole lightly hitting the helmet. These bits of information have been woven into the fabric of the scene, are essential to it, and so would have found themselves approved by Benjamin. The trees that day were green and there was the sound, for a few moments, in the midst of the rubble, and the crunching of the soldier's boots, of tapping. A story, which had sat waiting there, has been told. A very small story to be sure. But also a very beautiful one. Like something the great Robert Walser might have turned his attention to. Something like, as in one of Walser's sketches, one day an ordinary man, or a man who understands himself as ordinary, takes a tram ride and finds himself transformed into a king. Walser was writing about his present and now it comes to us as a gift about our past, which was not his past because he long ago died away from it, I thought, which seemed worth considering.

Indeed, in that context is there really any difference between writing about the present and writing about the past? I asked the Norfolk pine. The Norfolk pine and I were becoming fast friends on this journey to find the source of the ants. I appreciated its collegiality, if not its scratchiness, and told it so. The dead cat was still on the road when I walked by it in Cope and this made me think, without bitterness, of the fate of most of our endeavors, here on this earth. I still had some hope, had not yet begun to develop rationalizing strategies to cope, for my book about witches, that it might be read and thought about by a variety of people, possibly for years to come, and well into that tomorrow as I had been formulating it, but I had very quickly put hope behind me and soon it was the image of the dead cat, being crossed by what was starting to seem like an endless stream of leaf-cutter ants, that came to me when I thought of my book. Is that how I think of it now? Now that the publication has come and gone and my strategies for rationalizing its modest reception with it. "Il s'est passé quelque chose, mais pas grand-chose," is how my French editor might put it. And she might be right. Books decay in ways all their own. Some do it very quickly. No matter how nicely their information has been woven in or, for that matter, left entirely out. The Czech writer Bohumil Hrabal tells in his 1976 novella, *Too Loud a Solitude,* of a man whose job is to speed books on their way. His task is to compact wastepaper and discarded books into great bales in his basement workshop. The bales are composed of works large and small, remembered and half-remembered and forgotten, beautiful and strange and ugly and familiar. Sometimes Hanta, the narrator, places the work of a great philosopher or poet at the center of one of the bales. He describes moments of drunken (he loves beer) visionary bliss among these great cubes of crushed books and a feeling of solidarity with all the other dispossessed subterranean workers of Prague and an abiding interest in an epic battle between different-colored rats below the city streets. But there are also other kinds of moments, like the ones when the books and pages yet to be compacted become damp, miasmic, unredeemable, shit-smelling mush, or when the dump trucks drop off their papery contents and the air between Earth's surface and its underworld goes black for a few seconds with the uneven falling of unwanted pages and books from some former great repository, or when one of the trucks dumps sheet after sheet of bloody butcher paper into his cellar and the air fills up with flies. He says, at one juncture, "I could see how right Rimbaud was when he wrote that the battle of the spirit is as terrible as any armed conflict." Hrabal was writing in the context of the totalitarian purges that saw books disposed of by the millions and the ways in which, despite all, even their remains and wreckage can still spit gems, a dispensation that struck me—as I walked and thought about my own books and about decay and about how long it would be before my efforts and those of the writers who have lately meant a great deal to me were dumped out of the back of the truck into some cellar where a war among rats was being fought—as both grim and hopeful. *Who knows?* I thought, repeating it a few times and inserting a "the fuck" for good measure, and when I began seeing the Denver skyline off in the distance, I turned briefly, inconsequentially, more than a little bored by my preoccupations, to the question of relevance in determining the fate of one's work, which was, and still is, here in late 2019, and now here in early 2022, clearly the main criterion that obtains. Relevance of subject matter is good. Relevance of subject matter *and* of writer is better. So much better. It's an old formula. Subject to permutations. And of course it never, I thought in conclusion, hurts when someone is really good-looking.

A curious thing happened when I climbed the rise out of Superior and prepared to gaze down upon Boulder, which I had left just the day before, to see again its sprawl of lights lapping up against the bunched black mass of the Front Range: the ants and I kept climbing—or rather the ants were descending—as if rather than leveling off to plunge toward my home of sixteen years, the road they and I were traveling in different directions kept rising, invisible and steep, with a purpose all its own. Though not indefinitely for me, for when, huffing, I had climbed the unlooked-for rise alongside the leaf-cutter ants to a few hundred feet above the plunging road, which was a riot of Subarus and hybrids and trucks, I found I realized I was at the edge of a sheer drop. It was a cliff with my name on it that couldn't be seen, but which I took some satisfaction in having nonetheless, like the hole behind the door of the museum attendant's face, perceived. So I sat down with the Norfolk pine beside me, and dangled my legs off the edge, and watched the ants walking down out of the sky toward and past me and thought about all the days and weeks and months and years that had gone by, from a perspective I could never have hoped for, a view of what was now my past that let me see deep into the dark crenellations of the Front Range, and up through their twistings and sheerings to the stars where constituencies unlooked for surely lurked and where cliffs and singularities, whose openings might at any moment appear around any corner or curve and spew out infinite numbers of ants, abounded. Here then was the famous historical overview, and it was not inferred from a painting, or photograph, but from a stupid car stuck in the mud and a line of ants carrying chips of celestial leaves and my sorrow at leaving, which I have perhaps still not fully acknowledged, although I have tried and will keep trying still.

"'When love is in excess it brings a man no honor,' said Euripides," I said to the Norfolk pine. I said, "The past is impressionist, the present realist, and the future abstract." I said, "Three tenses is unsatisfying but at least they are better than two," but the Norfolk pine didn't answer, even though we were suspended, together, well above the earth and pointed, in postures of reverie, toward the stars. To the extent that for a moment I was confused because what I was hearing, having pushed the button, about the Red Cloud years of Willa Cather did not correspond with what I was thinking as, having returned, without paying as much attention to the ants this time, I walked back to where my car was stuck, across the fields and down the deceptive gravel road, out there in the north Kansas fields, in my vaguely Italian brown corduroy three-quarter-length jacket, which I have owned for ten years at least, and in my snug-leg Levi's and in my black-and-white dirt-covered Adidas Sambas, with the Norfolk pine under my arm. It did seem apparent to me, as the recording was clear to assert, that Willa Cather might very well have passed a pleasant part of her childhood, for it was good country, cut by clear water, covered by vastness of sky.

The attendant took even less notice of me as I left than she had when I walked in. The uniformed woman working at the convenience store I stopped at for water on my way out of town and up to the modest rigors of I-80 was inclined to offer me greater acknowledgment. I had not removed the large sign I had put under my windshield wiper when I was actually still a man in a brown corduroy jacket with his car stuck in the mud. The sign read, "Please Don't Steal Me." She raised an eyebrow and cocked her head and pursed her lips. Or did she purse her lips, lift her eyebrow, and cock her head? I told her my story, assured her it was my car when she expressed concern, pulled the key meaninglessly out of my pocket to show her, stopped short of pulling out my license too, discoursed a little about Willa Cather, said nothing about dangling my feet over invisible cliffs and talking to the plant because I hadn't thought of that yet and hurried back out. There were a couple of men at the gas pumps who had clearly also read the sign and were long-eyeing me. One of them had Don Henley's "The End of the Innocence" playing loudly in his pickup. That struck me as incongruous. This plus the woman's outsize suspicion and the slight flaring of the men's nostrils and remembering the various things I hadn't actually said to the Norfolk pine worked a kind of leavening tonic on my nerves and by the time I had made it up to I-80 I was laughing.

And while this laughter did not last very long, it did ease my passage onto that great northern artery, where trucks rule the rubber-smeared asphalt and people drive at high, uncomfortably fluctuating speed as they tithe carbon monoxide, nitrogen oxide, sulfur dioxide, hydrocarbons, and all variety of particulate matter into the overloaded donation plates of the sky. Listening to the Cure for a while helped, when the laughing curdled, as did listening to Duran Duran, the Talking Heads, the Bangles, and a-ha on the '80s station. I knew the lyrics to many of the songs I heard and sent Eleni and Eva crazed lip-synching videos that they were kind enough to find amusing if a little concerning. I went hard past Des Moines and Iowa City and kept hurtling east until I got to Ottawa, Illinois. The Fairfield Inn and Suites, located in the northern part of town, was a bigger, sprawlier affair than the Econo Lodge had been, and because my room was located deep in its guts, rather than right next to the parking lot, I had to do a great deal of ferrying things from the car, whose hatchback, unlike a trunk—a problem that had felt magnified on that muddy road in

Kansas—leaves little to the imagination. Twice after I thought I had gotten settled I remembered key items that were still in the car and so went back out for them. There was a wiry man of indeterminate age making lengthy preparations to spend the night in his van in the corner of the lot. I say lengthy because each time I went out he was still doing this and that outside his van. He moved with notable speed, and favored curtailed gestures, like he was agitated, and the last time I went out I had the feeling he was going to be up—doing calisthenics, brushing his teeth, buttoning up his shirt, taking it off, putting a different one on—late into the night. My room was both bland and overdone. I'm sorry to say I can't remember what books I had brought along to read. I think maybe there was one about Chaucer. I read *The Canterbury Tales* during freshman year in college. Likely I opened my computer and watched something on Netflix. Probably I double-checked to see that my Geiger counter was working. It had been a long day. I was exhausted. I slept.

Then woke early the next morning and, Geiger counter in hand, drove over to the Saint Columba Cemetery, where a number of the famous Radium Girls are buried. The Radium Girls earned their sobriquet by working at the Radium Dial Company, which was located in a former high school in downtown Ottawa from the early 1920s through the mid-1930s. Some of them also worked at Luminous Processes, Inc., another company opened by the same owner when the Radium Dial Company was shut down in the wake of negative press coverage related to lawsuits filed by certain of the girls whose teeth and jaws had inconveniently started to come loose. That the excruciating pain they also felt in their arms and legs and ankles, which was often accompanied by devastating nausea and crushing fatigue, and was too often followed by death, was ignored by the company is of course in no way surprising, given the long-standing, well-documented tradition that crosses all borders of international corporate malfeasance and depredation and blame shirking in the face of suffering by discounted peoples great and small. Companies have always done this. They are doing it right now and will continue to do it. I thought of this, and of the line managers who at least in the early days would eat spoonfuls of radium powder to show the young women, some of them truly little more than girls, that it was perfectly safe to ingest, even if there might be rumors to the contrary going around, as I stood above the grave of Ella Cruse, holding my Geiger counter close to the polished gray stone to see if it was true, as I had read, that all these years later she and the soil surrounding her were still hot. I thought, as I switched the small device on, of how the young women, who often kept bowls of candy within reach to counter the bitter taste of the powder, would dip their wet brushes into the powder, then "point" the tips in their mouths, then paint the numbers on the clock- and watch faces with the glowing isotope, which came home every night with them in their hair and on their clothes and in their mouths. There was a worker, who might have been cousin to the man I had seen in the parking lot at my hotel, or for that matter the man himself, mowing the grass near Ella Cruse's grave, so I tried to be discrete as I read the numbers, which confirmed that the radium that had gone to the grave with Ella Cruse, who died when she was twenty-four, was very much still burning away, as in a very real sense she still was, there below the earth I was standing on.

"Radium has a half-life of sixteen hundred years," I said to the Norfolk pine as I climbed into the car, having checked this with my phone as I leaned for a minute and looked out over the stones toward a nearby tree with an enormous chancre on its trunk, which was hard to believe, even if it must have been, was coincidental. "For some years," I said, "following its isolation by Pierre and Marie Curie during their research into pitchblende, radium was indeed considered not just harmless but actually salubrious. Glow-in-the-dark dining sets were made so that, presumably for novelty's sake, dinner parties could be hosted in limited-light environments, and soft, elastic yarn—Laine Oradium—was liberally treated with radium so that cozy onesies and jumpers could be knitted to keep your baby warm. Not *your* baby, of course," I said to the Norfolk pine. "Ella Cruse," I said, "might have been among the employees who were encouraged to take tins of radium paint home to decorate their houses with and she would have surely been spotted, on many an evening, glowing in the dusk light, maybe in company, as she made her way home."

"They were sometimes called Ghost Girls," I said as I began pulling out of the cemetery, saying it more to myself than to the Norfolk pine, which looked like it needed some water and which in truth wasn't as interesting to talk to when it was actually happening as opposed to when it wasn't. Talking to plants has a long history. Likely we have done it since the start. Of our talking, I mean. Our endless talking. There was a great deal of advocacy around it in the '70s and '80s when I was a boy. Talking to them will help them to grow and not talking to them will hurt them was the basic shot. You don't hear that as much these days. Or maybe it's just that I don't watch television the way I used to. "The shot" was an expression favored by my principal writing teacher in graduate school, Bobbie Louise Hawkins. She was now dead. By "now" I mean when I was pulling out of the cemetery, past the tree with the huge chancre and the glade of graves where Ella Cruse lay crackling.

I didn't have much other business to do in Ottawa, although I did want to see where the old death factory had stood, and to visit the recently erected memorial to the many who died. This should have been quick to accomplish but it wasn't. Street after street that my GPS was telling me would lead me to the site was blocked off. Police cars and fire trucks were everywhere. I spoke to a man in a weathered yellow ball cap that said "Paradise" on its front in faded red letters, who told me that a gas main had sprung a leak and that the downtown had been closed off and that I'd best do my visiting another day. Because I didn't have another day, I kept rattlesnaking my way forward. I say rattlesnaking rather than just snaking or garter snaking or vipering or fer-de-lancing because some of the bottles I was transporting were rattling as I made my turns. I passed beautiful old houses. No one was walking around, though other cars were out. I rolled down the window. There was a chemical smell in the air. It did not smell quite like sulfur, which is what I associate with leaking gas. It was easy to imagine the world Ella Cruse would have known by looking at the beautiful houses and handsome buildings and also by smelling death in the air. I can't say if it was the former or the latter that brought to mind a line of Walser's, who is clearly much on my mind these days, which can be found in a gathering of his feuilleton pieces called *Girlfriends, Ghosts, and Other Stories,* "Remember there is life and there is death, remember there are moments of bliss and there are graves."

Probably I should note that this was about a novel. That this visit to one of the towns associated with the Radium Girls of the 1920s and 1930s was about a book I wanted to write. I had already used some of the material in a short novel called *Zorrie* set in rural Indiana, which though not many people know it was a companion piece to an earlier novel of mine set in rural Indiana, but this was another book. A book I have not written. Or rather a book I wrote half of and set aside. This has been happening a lot lately. I keep running out of enthusiasm for my work, the air gets let out of the tires of my imagination and the ride feels mushy. It all keeps feeling thin. Ice you do not want to walk over. Pick your metaphor. I keep asking myself what the point is. This is new. I remember a few years ago a famous poet saying in a *New York Times* interview that male writers should stop writing. For fifty or a hundred years. Just quit. A lot of people have said similar things since then for reasons that make a lot of sense to me. I mean I get it. That's the problem. In a nutshell, as my grandmother would have added. I have a lot of respect for this poet, who is also a fabulous writer of fiction. So it sinks in. I wonder what Willa Cather would have said. Or Marguerite Yourcenar. Or Mata Hari. Somehow hearing it from Mata Hari would have hurt worse. Maybe it's because I've seen the place where she was shot, the wall outside Paris that she was made to stand against so that the bullets that flew through her would not fly any farther. Who was I to be thinking of writing the story of the young women whose lives were wrecked by radium anyway? Who was I to have written about women in the past? My eyes were beginning to burn. I found the memorial: a young dial painter holding the brush that probably killed her or wrecked her body and built its wreckage into her offspring if she had had any in one hand and a tulip in the other. The tulip did not look so good. You get what the artist was hoping to convey. *Les neiges d'antan* were killed by corporate greed and malfeasance. Where the plant stood nearby was a gaping foundation hole that was not terribly well blocked off. Any teenager with a can of spray paint and a pack of smokes could get into it for some hanging out. This was a couple of blocks away from the courthouse. The young woman in the statue was dressed in the style of the 1920s. Have I made it clear that they were mostly painting clockfaces to be used in the home and watch faces to be worn about town? That that is what it was all about?

I am writing and now revising this with a view of the Norfolk pine. It sits in the same green pot it crossed the country in by one of the front windows of our new house. It has done well here. Norfolk pines tend to do well and in this way they are good beginner plants. It's such a frondy, mellow creature. Are plants creatures? I do sometimes wonder that when I've had occasion to prune them. My wondering is not very important compared to the plant's wondering on this subject. I have not yet pruned the Norfolk pine. In truth it has been some while since I pruned anything other than the shrub plums and shrub cherries in our back yard in the house on Edinboro Drive that we no longer live in. I am not much of a pruner though in my day I was pretty good with an electric trimmer and once trimmed the evergreens around my great aunt and uncle's house with a chainsaw. Nor am I much given to spritzing or watering appropriately. In fact, I don't have much of a green thumb at all. There are other plants in pots near the Norfolk pine, including a snake plant. Now, the snake plant is an impressive thing. It's a whole small green forest of green spears. You would not say that about the Norfolk pine. We have little Meyer lemon trees too. Eleni makes marmalade with their fruit. She is the one with the green thumb. Outside the window are bushes and trees. Below the ground, where the cramped roots of the Norfolk pine and the snake plant and the Meyer lemon trees can't reach, is the great mycelial network that fills the soil of the earth with its own burn, its own glow.

And it was the thought of this great connective rubric whose intentions we do not understand that more than anything took parry thrusts at my mind as I climbed on top of my car and closed my eyes and improvised a small song of parting to the Radium Girls who stopped glowing long ago but will continue to burn about the bone when the little we have understood about being alive and human has been forgotten or replaced, then went back to the hotel to retrieve my belongings and got back onto I-80 to continue east. In a proper story—the kind I don't much like to read anymore but still often admire—I would have found something to say about the man I had seen the night before and thought I might have seen again in the cemetery pushing a lawnmower but his van was gone when I went to check out and the truth is I kind of forgot about him. Or maybe it's just that this story too is running out of steam. Once, in Costa Rica, our guide in the cloud forest asked me what exactly the point of *One Hundred Years of Solitude* had been. He had read the whole thing and just hadn't gotten it and thought that perhaps I, as someone who wrote myself and taught writing, might be able to help. We were bouncing down from the cool, rainy forest. We had just seen a motmot bird on a fence. He had been pointing out the monkey "bridges" that went over the roads and somehow books had come up. I said something about the textures of lived experience, the weaving and unweaving of human lives and memories as they carry out their journeys, long and short, and how things extraordinary sometimes explode out of this, which sounded pretty good, and seemed actually to help, if he wasn't just being nice, but now I'm not so sure. What, beyond the stuff you can say in thirty seconds on an ungraded mountain road, is *One Hundred Years of Solitude* about and what is *Memoirs of Hadrian* about and what is *Dhalgren* about and *Erasure* and *Beloved* and *The Sun Also Rises* and *The Waves*? That book is both tedious as fuck and so fabulous it can make your eyes water and I mean at the same time. I'm not sure why I felt I needed to say that. I was following a line of thought and then stepped away and when I came back it was gone. A movie I kind of liked called *Iceman,* about the famous Stone Age man found frozen in the Tyrolean Alps, takes the core of that gesture as its prime mover. A man steps away for a hunt and when he gets back his family is dead and his village is burning. One moment it is all there and you can see where you are going and where you have been and the next it is all gone. Much like those famous breadcrumbs in the forest. If only dear Hansel and dear Gretel had been able to grow wings and fly after the birds and eat them in turn.

I have no memory of the birds I saw as I flew east across northern Indiana, Ohio, Pennsylvania, and New York. They were there of course. Just as there were birds on the prairies of Willa Cather's childhood and on the glowing streets of Ottawa, Illinois, when young Ella Cruse, already in her final years, was heading home from work. Here in Providence there are doves and pigeons and starlings and sparrows and chickadees and Carolina wrens and Cooper's hawks and geese and cardinals and blue jays and swans. In Costa Rica there were scarlet macaws and motmots and summer tanagers and parakeets and purple hummingbirds and clay-colored thrushes and gray-necked wood rails and egrets and kingfishers and frigate birds and black hawks and turkey vultures and peacocks and quetzals. We saw one of these latter flying over a chasm. We saw the tail feathers of another sticking out of the cave of its nest. We heard an ornate hawk eagle flying over the canopy near Drake Bay on the Osa Peninsula but did not see it. This was in the future. Of my drive east. The future, which I've now heartbeaten into the past, even as I made my way through the heavy rain along the Massachusetts Turnpike, and crossed the sky bridges, in luminous layered textures. All our hearts were beating as we barreled down the highway. Those of us with hearts. Those of us still there.

# GOD BLESS JOHNNY CASH

After the long drive east was over and the move complete, when I pressed my thumb and my middle finger against my temples, then pulled slowly inward over the tops of my eyebrows, I pressed and pulled hard. My temples and eyebrows, and the ascending line of ridges that formed when I pressed in and up, were smeared and beaded with sweat as often as not and more than once I caused that familiar blend of water, ammonia, urea, salt, and sugar to drip onto my nose and around onto the lower edge of my nostril, which made me sneeze. That this stress-relieving mechanism should only be put into practice by me for the first time during the summer of my fiftieth year as I drove or rode my bike around Providence, Rhode Island, or walked across the box-strewn rooms of our new house on Freeman Parkway, was surprising because I have long fallen prey to stress, long been easy meat for the tongue of its attention, the appraisal of its sharp, probing teeth.

It was not clear to me, because I felt stressed all the time as the summer of 2018 inched toward autumn, that the cousin actions of pressing and pulling were doing much in the way of offering relief, but they may have been. I did notice that my eczema, which in recent years had taken to blooming like blotched red algae whenever life turned to challenge, behaved itself a little better after I had taken up this highly specific form of automassage, and I did not, it seems to me, subsequently clench my teeth and growl about the small things as much as I might otherwise have. Sometimes after I had pressed and before I began to pull I would tense the back of my neck and press the contact points of my skull into my fingers. This was a variant. A kind of optional independent clause to the central thrust of the sentence taking shape along my brow. As too was slowly moving my jaw back and forth and breathing in unquietly through my nose. The main thing though was the pressing and the pulling, which when repeated, as it inevitably was, and sometimes several times, put me in mind first of a grounded flock of black-webbed geese I saw slapping the asphalt along the ragged edge of a local bridge that, one morning, took me out and over the Seekonk River, and now, here in the winter of 2022, of the proliferation of discarded gloves that characterized the early days of the coronavirus pandemic.

And though it seems so far from inevitable that I am tempted to doubt the authenticity of the association, that image of geese diverted, perhaps forever, from their right way, bills as darkly iridescent as their feet, and that of endless gloves stripped forever from their hands, gloves worn, I now recall, at least in part to remind us never to touch our faces and so infect ourselves, has made me think more and more of the so-called Black Paintings by Francisco Goya. These fascinating, frightening works were found directly painted on and subsequently extracted from the walls of Goya's country house, La Quinta del Sordo, long after his death. Painted originally onto the walls of the lower and upper floors of the house, these paintings, which have long lived in the Prado, where they are seen by millions each year, depict solitary dogs, satanic gatherings, murderous fathers, wicked smiles, and astonished onlookers, who, it is the easiest thing in the world to imagine, will at any moment link arms and go dancing, with good appetite, toward some gruesome—perhaps plague-inflicted—death. If I, following convention, at first mention attribute these famous works to the world-renowned court painter of Charles IV, their provenance is apparently not fully settled. This has as much to do with key stylistic differences from Goya's public-facing work as it has to do with questions—raised in the early 2000s by Juan José Junquera, a professor of art history at Complutense University of Madrid—about the physical composition of the Deaf Man's House. According to Junquera's research, the second floor of the structure, where a number of the paintings were found, was added after Goya's death. Meaning someone else painted them.

Because he studied painting, though never showed his own efforts, knew his father's work, and had access to the house after the great painter had left it, Goya's son Javier strikes Junquera as the most likely candidate. And even if some as-yet-undiscovered piece of correspondence puts Goya the elder back in the house after he left it and indeed Spain entirely to retire to France, or some other document clearly establishes their existence before his departure, it's intriguing to imagine that Javier, the only one of Goya's many sons to reach adulthood, and who appears to have lived an unremarkable life, one day took up the brushes he had long since abandoned in favor of a career in business, and using his father's former walls as canvas, made something remarkable.

Looked at through the lens of our current preoccupation with authenticity and, for many, the indisputable autobiographical connection between a work and its creator, we could well imagine that the aging Spaniard, utterly eclipsed by the adjacent immortality of his father, intended to represent his own brutalized self in that grisly paternal embrace offered by Saturn. Or that the dog in the bottom left of another painting is none other than him, Javier, small and alone on the cloudy slopes of the cosmos. Or that he, Javier, attended a satanic gathering and sat gleefully cackling at the feet of a goat-headed sorcerer. Who knows?

There is a portrait by Goya that may or may not be of Javier. In it a young man is wearing a brown suit and weeps vulnerability from every crease. Young as the subject is, he will nonetheless, it pleases me to think, have lifted his fingers to his own forehead and pressed and pulled before and after each sitting. Or perhaps he wrung his hands. Or shivered involuntarily. Which is something I have done frequently for years. It strikes me at strange moments. My teenaged daughter finds it funny and vaguely alarming—her father suddenly jerking his shoulders and wriggling his arms. I do it more of late. For example when I conduct an internet search for "COVID Providence" or "COVID New York City" or "COVID Greece" or "COVID India" or "COVID Japan" or "COVID USA" or "COVID World."

No one said whether or not the black vulture on display at the local Audubon Society's annual Raptor Fest we attended in our first year in Rhode Island had his own idiosyncrasies, his own individual markers of destiny; the presenters only described what the characteristics of his species were. His bill was long so it could be plunged deep into a carcass. His stomach could process anything, even anthrax, and certainly a humble coronavirus variant or two. He had a funny name, which of course would have been utterly unknown to him, and just sat there quietly—unlike the bald eagle who came out later and for a short while created a hurricane beside his handler's head—on a gloved forearm, looking at us. Perhaps to see if we would stop moving. And stay stopped there in our chairs for a long enough time.

My daughter, Eva, who is nonetheless a big reader, hasn't yet read *The Red Pony* by John Steinbeck, which so vividly ends its opening section in a circling of big, long-beaked birds. If she ever does read it, I don't know what she will think about the killing of the vulture who has begun his feast by pulling out one of the beloved dead pony's eyes, but perhaps she will feel, as Steinbeck allows, the injustice of it. The vulture is doing its job just as the dead pony is doing its new job, which is to be dead, to allow for the dissemination of its flesh, to feed the bacteria and insects and larger animals that will come. Who knows where its atoms, locked but fizzing during the years of their service in his body, will go now that they are no longer needed. Do they mourn in some sense as they melt or are absorbed by bacteria or are taken up by long black beaks? Flesh is mortal.

Atoms, we like to think, are not. At least not in any way that would be recognizable to ponies and people.

The short essay "Ash, Needle, Pencil, and Match" by Robert Walser, which I first read in fine translation by a former student of mine named Shawn Huelle, continues to seem to me to be all about flesh though the word appears nowhere in its brief pages. Ash gathers and disperses, the needle pierces, the poor little pencil tries to keep up, and the matchstick "weeps fire" and torches it all. Walser, who spent many years in an asylum, and was found dead one Christmas morning in a snowdrift after a walk, would have had his own stress procedures and protocols, though it seems reasonable to imagine that the dark fizz of nerves and pronounced occlusion of the breathing apparatus and crisping of heart and lips was differently languaged in that earlier age.

The gentleman is fatigued, one might have said. The gentleman is irritable. The gentleman is nervous. The gentleman is tense. The gentleman would like to go back to his room. The gentleman would like a dry handkerchief. The gentleman has a toothache. Please call the doctor: the gentleman's stomach is upset. Nurse, the gentleman requires fresh bedding. The gentleman is suffocating. The gentleman is experiencing a sensation of drowning. The gentleman has no appetite. The gentleman has had a dream about his mother. In the dream his mother is lying in her bed. It is the middle of the afternoon and the gentleman, dressed in short pants and a school tie, carefully approaches. There are no lights on in the room. The curtains are drawn. The gentleman in short pants goes closer. The mother has her head under a pillow. He must go very close in order to be able to see if she is still breathing. Is she still breathing? The dream doesn't tell the gentleman. The dream won't allow him to get close enough. There he stands in his short pants. When he wakes he has an unassuageable craving for candy.

Javier Goya would have called it something different too. When he felt that way. When he wanted sweets. And couldn't breathe fully, properly. Couldn't take in long deep gulps of gorgeous air. Which of course is what COVID-19 and its various variants take from one. From you. The body's beautiful ability to draw nourishment from the air. Perhaps he—if it is him in that portrait—has just been scolded by his tyrannical father. Or has failed in another business dealing. Or has lost another argument with a hulking neighbor. Or has woken up from another terrible dream. He was, or—if it isn't him in the portrait—would have been, better dressed at the very least, the young businessman with the famous father who had studied painting, than the old Swiss writer found in a shabby suit and threadbare coat in a snowdrift. Merry Christmas, Herr Walser. Merry Christmas, Javier.

I know nothing about nineteenth-century Spain.

Or early twentieth-century Switzerland.

I know nothing about late twentieth-century America or early twenty-first-century America though I live here and have my opinions.

Opinions are not literature.

Or are they?

Maybe now. Maybe so.

Henry James in his famous objection to historical fiction, which he set out in a letter of dissuasion to Sarah

Orne Jewett, who had sent him a copy of her new book, asserts that because one could never hope—as one could with one's present—to capture the past's subtle folds and minute textures, the high-thread-count fabric of vanished consciousness one should not write about days gone by at all.

Thank God Hilary Mantel didn't get the memo. Or Toni Morrison. Or Louise Erdrich. Or Cormac McCarthy. Or Edward P. Jones. Or Selah Saterstrom. Best not to, my dear. Don't do it, my darling. That musty old emperor doesn't need your help. Let Natchez sleep. Holster that pen. Put away your paper. I feel richly about my moment and you should too. Watch me now. Watch me go all granular on the subject of memes and tweets and what they do to the twenty-first-century soul. I will sound the deep caverns of emotion I and my lightly fictionalized avatars are feeling about post-cubicle culture, iPhone vs. Samsung (is that still a thing?), and convenience marts.

Take my hand. Hold me tight. My moment is rushing. It roars through me. I can feel it all.

Johnny Cash felt it all. You can feel it in his songs. From start to finish this feeling-it-all is there. Listen to "So Doggone Lonesome" and you can hear it. Listen to "Ring of Fire" and hear it. Listen to his late-life cover of "Hurt" by Nine Inch Nails. The needle tears a hole. The hole opens into a burning ring he had fallen into years before. The empire of dirt was always around. Bob Dylan may well have claimed to catch the body of his times by the neck, but the man in black had already hooked his own hand there and hadn't let go.

My second-favorite fire song is Leonard Cohen's 1974 "Who by Fire." That feels important to interject. It also feels important to add that if Dylan had his times by the neck Leonard Cohen had his hand on their cheek. Oh, Leonard Cohen. Oh, to gently touch fingertips to the cheek of your times. I don't care if you feel differently. About Leonard Cohen I mean. Neil Young's "Harvest" puts me in an analogous space. He sang it in London in 1971. I am listening to the recording now. At one moment you can hear someone coughing in the background. Who coughed? All of us and one of us. What a marvelous thing to hear behind all that lovely, wobbly, immortal warble.

It's possible Dylan never quite claimed to have put his hand around his era's neck. He says something like that in his *Chronicles*. It's a grand claim, however he made it, and probably true. What is also true is that if you want to send my aforementioned sixteen-year-old into paroxysms of rage you will put Bob Dylan's Christmas album on when the tree lights are lit and the eggnog is poured and the weather outside is frightful. Remind her in such a context of how amazing Bob Dylan was and is and will be long after any of us are still around and she might smash the stereo.

What would make me smash the stereo?

REO Speedwagon maybe. Air Supply certainly. Basically that ghastly soft shit that afflicted the '80s of my youth.

"So it goes."

My shuttle driver from the car repair shop a few weeks ago was a masked elderly man named Gus who told me he had lived in Providence for forty-seven years. This was after leaving the Madeira Islands. He referred to them as the Madeira Islands *in* Portugal. And so I suppose they are, both in law and in the mental architecture of a man who still speaks with a heavy accent and stays tuned to a local Portuguese radio station when he drives the company van through the streets of a disease-afflicted city that has been his home for half a century. He spoke of the beauty of the islands and of the Azores and of Lisbon, old and proud. He told me more than once that every hour the station, which broadcasts out of New Bedford, gave highlights of the news back home. He had a tender way of speaking both about Portugal and about the weather "and mess" around us, over which—because it was all decided upstairs—we had no control. He said he wished more people would remember that it was all in good hands and that we didn't need to worry so much about things in general. The pandemic would pass. It would one day be done. The Big Guy had our back. The Big Guy, maybe more importantly, had his mask on. Gus had a theory that because there were so many of us alive at the same time now, all our worrying, which disregarded the Big Guy's sacred covenant to us, billowed up like dark clouds that "sometimes blocked up" all the goodness of His sunshine.

I saw Gus again when my car was ready for pickup. We did not speak this time about the beautiful islands of Portugal as there were new COVID numbers out as well as numerous small eccentricities of traffic to be commented upon as we made our way through the East Side streets and over the bridge, where I kept my eyes peeled for geese but saw none. There were swans out on the water though. Six of them I thought, though the last one I counted may have just been a bit of bend and flash of midwinter light. Are there swans on the Madeira Islands? Are there geese?

These unasked questions and others brought me spinning back through space to the endless games of *Adventure* and *Asteroids* I used to play on the Atari set I had in my room at my grandmother's house in rural Indiana. So that as I thanked Gus and watched him pull away and went into the office to pay, I was thinking of sitting hunched and cross-legged on the plush rose-colored carpet on the third floor of the farmhouse built by my great-grandparents in 1913. I inserted my credit card into the credit card machine and signed the papers required and collected my key and all the while I was sitting there, joystick in hand, trying desperately to fight off the asteroids—which seem to me now to have had a distinctly viral aspect—that came at the little triangle of my ship from multiple directions and with ever-greater speed. I got back into my car and started it and began to make my way home and still I was sitting there, alone on the third floor, fighting with little skill to defend the triangle that was me. Every now and again a flying saucer would also go on the attack. The tinny sounds were deeply satisfying to me as I sat there, though the inertial drift of hitting the thrusters was disturbing as always. My mother was in Baltimore and my father was far away getting a new life going in Taiwan. I didn't know it yet but I would never live with either of them again. On balance, I was not that good at Asteroids. When the triangle was struck it broke into messy bits of light. This happened thousands of times.

I looked for the swans and geese yesterday when I went over the Waterman bridge, but saw only cars and sky and winter grass and leafless trees and derelict buildings and deep water, which, if I had the strength and knew my course, I could travel over or under all the way to the Madeira Islands, about which H. N. Coleridge, nephew of the poet, apparently opined, "I should think the situation of Madeira the most enviable on the whole earth." There perhaps I could make the acquaintance of other soft-spoken, mask-wearing people like Gus and take long walks along the striking cliffs and through the lovely forests and sip fine Madeira wine and never need to stand in shorts beside the bed of bad feeling again. In the Madeira Islands, even if the coronavirus couldn't be fended off, the stomach of the mind could digest anything and the triangle would never be made to burst into bits of quick-fading color. The author of *Jakob von Gunten* would never fall over into the snow. Saturn would never pick up his son and bite off his head.

A police car put on its lights and siren and pulled up fast behind me.

Probably it's panic I've been talking about, not stress. Panic, Mr. Walser. Panic, Javier. Panic, little dog.

# STILL LIFE WITH SNOW AND HAMMER

*The emotions he experienced seemed to have taken hold
of the deepest roots and subtlest fibers of his being. And
so much the more that it was so subterranean in him, so
much the more did he feel its weird inscrutableness.*
—*Herman Melville,* Pierre; or, The Ambiguities

One snowy night in my early days, I was out playing on
the street with a large green-handled hammer. My game
was to stand in the middle of the quiet street and throw
the hammer up into the dark, snow-filled air and to let
it fall with a pleasantly muffled *thunk* onto the ground.
Before long, I was joined by another, equally young
individual, one I was in the habit of exchanging blows
with, and, after wrestling around a little, by whatever
mysterious alchemy of adrenaline and alliance that can
still take place at that age, we took to standing at opposite ends of the street and flinging the hammer back and
forth. To the peculiarly delicious pleasure to be had in
launching a hard and heavy object up into the air and
waiting for it to fall were consequently added the ele-
ments of targeting, trajectory, and return. And it is of

the latter aspect that I think especially these strange, grim days. This is because it wasn't very long before, like the lovely knuckleheads we were, we took to standing directly under the point of the hammer's projected descent only to leap out of its way at the last second, with the idea that points were to be awarded for the nearest misses and that the game would be over when one or the other of us was hit. A car door slammed, someone's mother rapped meaningfully on a window, I'm not sure—my attention wavered and I got hit, smacked hard on the arm. Pride demanded that I sue for another round. He then, having been winged on the calf, said it could only be settled by going best out of three. We stood there a moment before the final exchange started, sizing each other up, breathing hard. Then he yelled something and I yelled something back and threw. Minutes elapsed as the hammer flew back and forth between us. I believe it had begun to snow harder. We had both achieved the kind of high-pitched frenzy that is not always but can be accompanied by a great deal of shrieking and hopping around. So it was that at the end of the longest and final round, I stood under the looping, falling hammer, looking up into the dark, snowy air with a mixture of terror and exaltation, as well as a sense of unreality, as if it weren't me about to be hit on the head by a carpenter's hammer, as if there were no snow, as if it weren't night. Stupid boy, poor child, my mother said. Suddenly, years and years have passed.

# NOTES

Tiger [Tiger] Tiger

# UN Story

# Giraffe Story

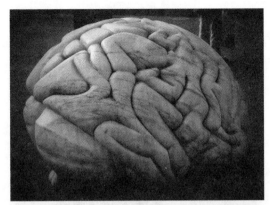

# Half Moon (a provisional fiction)

# Climb the Whale

God Bless Johnny Cash

# Still Life with Snow and Hammer

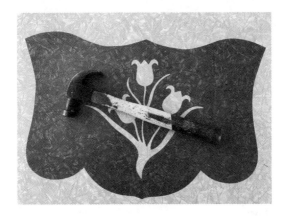

The author would like to thank the editors of *Plume, Conjunctions, L'école de littérature* (ecoledelitterature.blogspot .com), *Western Humanities Review,* and *110 Stories: New York Writes after September 11,* where earlier versions of some of these pieces first appeared.

Coffee House Press began as a small letterpress operation in 1972 and has grown into an internationally renowned nonprofit publisher of literary fiction, essay, poetry, and other work that doesn't fit neatly into genre categories.

Coffee House is both a publisher and an arts organization. Through our *Books in Action* program and publications, we've become interdisciplinary collaborators and incubators for new work and audience experiences. Our vision for the future is one where a publisher is a catalyst and connector.

# FUNDER ACKNOWLEDGMENTS

Coffee House Press is an internationally renowned independent book publisher and arts nonprofit based in Minneapolis, MN; through its literary publications and *Books in Action* program, Coffee House acts as a catalyst and connector—between authors and readers, ideas and resources, creativity and community, inspiration and action.

Coffee House Press books are made possible through the generous support of grants and donations from corporations, state and federal grant programs, family foundations, and the many individuals who believe in the transformational power of literature. This activity is made possible by the voters of Minnesota through a Minnesota State Arts Board Operating Support grant, thanks to the legislative appropriation from the Arts and Cultural Heritage Fund. Coffee House also receives major operating support from the Amazon Literary Partnership, Jerome Foundation, Literary Arts Emergency Fund, McKnight Foundation, and the National Endowment for the Arts (NEA). To find out more about how NEA grants impact individuals and communities, visit www.arts.gov.

Coffee House Press receives additional support from Bookmobile; Dorsey & Whitney LLP; Elmer L. & Eleanor J. Andersen Foundation; the Matching Grant Program Fund of the Minneapolis Foundation; Mr. Pancks' Fund in memory of Graham Kimpton; the Schwab Charitable Fund; and the U.S. Bank Foundation.

## THE PUBLISHER'S CIRCLE OF
## COFFEE HOUSE PRESS

Publisher's Circle members make significant contributions to Coffee House Press's annual giving campaign. Understanding that a strong financial base is necessary for the press to meet the challenges and opportunities that arise each year, this group plays a crucial part in the success of Coffee House's mission.

Recent Publisher's Circle members include many anonymous donors, Patricia A. Beithon, Anitra Budd, Andrew Brantingham, Kelli & Dave Cloutier, Mary Ebert & Paul Stembler, Kamilah Foreman, Jocelyn Hale & Glenn Miller Charitable Fund of the Minneapolis Foundation, the Rehael Fund-Roger Hale/Nor Hall of the Minneapolis Foundation, Randy Hartten & Ron Lotz, Dylan Hicks & Nina Hale, William Hardacker, Kenneth & Susan Kahn, the Kenneth Koch Literary Estate, Cinda Kornblum, Jennifer Kwon Dobbs & Stefan Liess, the Lenfestey Family Foundation, Sarah Lutman & Rob Rudolph, the Carol & Aaron Mack Charitable Fund of the Minneapolis Foundation, Gillian McCain, Mary & Malcolm McDermid, Daniel N. Smith III & Maureen Millea Smith, Enrique & Jennifer Olivarez, Robin Preble, Nan G. Swid, Grant Wood, and Margaret Wurtele.

For more information about
the Publisher's Circle and other ways
to support Coffee House Press books,
authors, and activities, please visit
www.coffeehousepress.org/pages/donate or
contact us at info@coffeehousepress.org.

**LAIRD HUNT** is the author of *Zorrie*, which was a 2021 finalist for the National Book Award in Fiction. He has also been a finalist for the PEN/Faulkner Award for Fiction and won the Anisfield-Wolf Award for Fiction, the Grand Prix de Littérature Américaine, and Italy's Bridge Prize. His reviews and essays have been published in the *New York Times*, the *Washington Post*, the *Los Angeles Times*, and many others. He teaches in the Department of Literary Arts at Brown University and lives in Providence.

*This Wide Terraqueous World* was designed by
Bookmobile Design & Digital Publisher Services.
Text is set in Mrs Eaves.